HAMMARSKJÖLD

The Political Man

BY THE SAME AUTHOR

The Indian Round Table Conference
Platypus at Large
Peace in Their Time
The Political Playtpus
Hammarskjöld

UN CHILDREN'S BOOKS
The Valley of Trust
Food for the Valley
UN Coloring Book
Proverbs of Many Nations
Peace is an Adventure
Stamps Tell the Story of the UN

IN COLLABORATION WITH A. DERSO
Guignol à Lausanne
Les Guardiens de la Paix
La Bourse de Paris
Debt and Reparations
Le Testament de Genève
The League at Lunch

HAMMARSKJÖLD

The Political Man

EDITED BY EMERY KELEN

Funk & Wagnalls, New York

TO MY WIFE, BETTY

"To the diplomat of the middle of the twentieth century, war is something that must be averted at almost any cost."

—Hammarskjöld

Contents

The Bridge Builder

In times of mortal danger, it is natural that man should seek shelter in fatalistic mysticism. Dag Hammarskjöld's tragic death and the publication of his secret diary, Markings, which revealed his profound excursions into a world not governed by politics, attracted the attention of more people than ever listened to his remarks on mundane matters. It only goes to prove once again that a dead martyr is worth ten living saints, but one regrets nevertheless the death of a martyr, wondering what work he would have done had he lived.

In the minds of many, Hammarskjöld has become almost a religious figure, and it is sometimes forgotten that he was above all the Secretary-General of the United Nations, and one of the most clairvoyant political thinkers of our time, whose thoughts were shaped by an outstanding and cultivated intellect and founded on transcendent morality. He occupied a diplomatic post which not only put him in the position to know what he was talking about, but demanded that he speak and act dispassionately, detached from ideological and national bias. In short, he was a unique political accident.

It is therefore important for us to understand his ideas: what he thought about nuclear danger, disarmament, our divided world, and the new nations; and to know what sort of World Organization he envisaged.

The political Hammarskjöld was not eloquent, and he had not a trace of the common touch that enabled Roosevelt, Churchill, and Kennedy to capture the attention of large masses. Accustomed as he was to talking to lawyers and economists, some of his most significant speeches read like documents. It is hard to find the message behind the palisade of legalistic precisions. Yet his message is there, clear, cold, and deep as a tarn in the high mountains.

In his spectacular attempt to breathe life and strength into the United Nations Charter, Hammarskjöld drew upon his head all sorts of accusations: He was called a "megalomaniac"; a "dangerous man out to wreck the United Nations"; and "idealist" who was "out of step with reality."

But what is reality? If it is considered to be a static thing, a collection of facts that you can see in front of your nose, then reality is but a set of outdated shibboleths, and our policies are quite properly frozen in conformity to them. Hammarskjöld, however, did not regard reality as static, but as a climate in a perpetual state of motion and change, driven by dynamic forces such as mass movements, mass communications, and mass self-interest, as well as by our new access to enormous constructive and destructive resources. He was extremely sensitive to the new self-awareness of peoples the world over. For him everything was in a state of becoming, and so boldly did his mind arc to comprehend this process that stale reality had no part in his thinking.

If he was out of step with reality, therefore, it was yesterday's reality, not today's or tomorrow's. His grasp of the fleeting moment was sometimes called "uncanny perception" and it baffled those about him who were prisoners of conformism.

In human affairs, they say, there are the doers and the dreamers. There are also the bridge-builders, with a grasp of what is becoming; men like Lincoln, Woodrow Wilson, Pope John XXIII, and Gandhi. Hammarskjöld belongs in this company. He looked beyond confusion toward the germination of a new state of affairs. His opinions are profound, perhaps prophetic, and at all events salutary; it is well worth pondering what he had to say about the problems that trouble our minds.

Winter 1968

EMERY KELEN

HAMMARSKJÖLD

The Political Man

1

The United Nations

"We the peoples of the United Nations, determined to save succeeding generations from the scourge of war which twice in our lifetime has brought untold sorrow to mankind. . . ." Thus begins the United Nations Charter. When these words were written, the Second World War was still in progress. The atom bomb had not yet been dropped—indeed, the authors of the Charter did not know of its existence; still, the "untold sorrow" had already been brought home to the world.

"This great Organization," said Dag Hammarskjöld before the General Assembly in 1953, "grew out of the pain and turmoil of the last war. It welded together in what should be a continued cooperation for world peace all those who had fought against oppression. By all who have sacrificed themselves, by all sacrificing themselves in the fight for freedom and peace. . . ."

Hammarskjöld did not look upon the United Nations as a panacea or as a superstate which could dictate solutions, or even as a creator of politics: He looked upon it—and indeed helped to forge it—as an instrument added to the technique of diplomacy. A World Organization was not a new idea, he pointed out; it was a logical development from lines of thought that had begun the first time a few men began to think about the decency and dignity of other men. It was the embodiment of an ideal, a recognition that the use of force in any form as a means of

3

settling international disputes must be rejected, and that society must be founded on the principles of law, justice, and human rights.

While he was fully aware that the United Nations predated the use of nuclear energy and space travel, he did not on that account judge it to be outmoded. On the contrary, he thought that the Organization gained in significance from these developments, and he told the United States Governors Conference in 1958: "Its necessity as a venture in international cooperation is more clear today than when it was founded."

With all of its shortcomings, he saw no alternative to the World Organization. "We can improve on it . . . we can try and find new means to meet the needs, but . . . it must be on the same basis."

⟨ The United Nations organization remains the only universal agency in which countries with widely differing political institutions and at different stages of economic development may exchange views, share their problems and experiences, probe each other's reactions to policies of mutual interest, and initiate collective action; it is inspired and bound by the solemn pledge of the Charter to take "joint" as well as "separate" action. [51]*

⟨ Ideology. The word is a little dangerous, especially when we come to a body now composed of seventy-six Member States, representing all shades of ideas, philosophies, and religions. But, all the same, I feel that there is something that might be called United Nations ideology, a United Nations ideology which is very much alive for everybody who is working in and for the Organization, and, I can say, very much alive also for that famous "man in the street." [8]

⟨ As a universal organization neutral in the Big Power struggles over ideology and influence in the world, subordinated to the

*Numbers in parentheses refer to sources (pp. 232–236).

common will of the Member governments, and free from any aspirations of its own to power and influence over any group or nation, the United Nations can render service which can be received without suspicion and which can be absorbed without influencing the free choice of the peoples. [18]

❲ A weakening of the Organization, resulting from an attempt to achieve results at the cost of principles, is a loss not only for the future but also immediately in respect of the significance of the Organization for the vast majority of nations and in respect of their confidence in the Organization on which its strength in our present-day world ultimately depends. [18]

❲ The community of nations, represented in the United Nations, has a vital interest in a peaceful solution, based on justice, of any question which, unless brought to a satisfactory solution, might come to represent a threat to peace and security. [19]

❲ This Organization has—in the words of one of the greatest leaders of democracy—been "consecrated far above our poor power to add or detract." May I quote also these other words from the Gettysburg address. "The world will little note, nor long remember, what we say here, but it can never forget what they did. . . . It is for us, the living, rather to be dedicated here to the unfinished task which they have, thus far, so nobly advanced. It is rather for us to be here dedicated to the great task remaining before us." [21]

❲ Read in the right spirit, the Charter of the United Nations expresses an approach to the political problems of man which would have been well understood by men like Jefferson and Lincoln. [23]

❲ The principles of the Charter are, by far, greater than the Organization in which they are embodied, and the aims which they are to safeguard are holier than the policies of any single nation or people. [33]

⟪ It is not, and it can never be, a question of the United Nations living so to say, outside the Big Five, or being maintained somehow independently of the Big Five. It is necessarily a question of "both—and." I have already, I think, on some occasion indicated the need to have a balance between a recognition of the crucial role of the major powers, on the one side, and the rights and responsibilities of the majority of nations, on the other side. What I see as the future of the United Nations lies in the direction of such a balance. [61]

⟪ The greatest need today is to blunt the edges of conflict among the nations, not to sharpen them. If properly used, the United Nations can serve a diplomacy of reconciliation better than other instruments available to the Member states. All the varied interests and aspirations of the world meet in its precincts upon the common ground of the Charter. [38]

⟪ A failure to gain respect for decisions or actions of the Organization within the terms of the Charter is often called a failure for the Organization. It would seem more correct to regard it as a failure of the world community, through its Member nations and in particular those most directly concerned, to cooperate in order, step by step, to make the Charter a living reality in practical action as it is already in law. [19]

⟪ Service of the United Nations . . . whether it bears immediate fruit or not, whether it paves one more inch of the road ahead, one is more than rewarded by what is achieved. This is true whatever setbacks may follow: if a mountain wall is once climbed, later failures do not undo the fact that it has been shown that it can be climbed. In this sense, every step forward in the pioneer effort of this Organization inevitably widens the scope for the fight for peace. [15]

⟨ The United Nations is the means to an end, not an end in itself. [17]

⟨ The Organization was born out of the cataclysms of the Second World War. It should justify the sacrifices of all fighters for freedom and justice in that war. I remember the bitter lines of a great Anglo-American poet [W. H. Auden] who writes in an "Epitaph on an Unknown Soldier":

> *To save your world, you asked this man to die,*
> *Would this man, could he see you now, ask why?*

⟨ The United Nations is what the Member nations make it. [27]

2

The Nation and the World

Two emotion-charged words prominent in our discussions of everyday affairs — "nationalism" and "internationalism" — prompted Hammarskjöld to speculative thinking and an attempt at clarification and definition. It seemed to him that the teachings of Christ tended to internationalism; but although Western man has honored these teachings for two millennia; throughout that time, "nationalism in the narrow and dangerous sense of the word has remained a major force."

Hammarskjöld thought that we must teach ourselves to overcome "a nationalism which seeks its own gratification at the expense of others or which aims at increased power or territorial expansion." Yet he saw a nobler side to it, not necessarily opposed to internationalism, but rather an incubator for more mature political views. "National feeling can be also harmoniously merged with the feeling of international responsibility. Nations in free contact with the world can develop their special qualities and assets which should give them their just weight in international balance. They could manifest and protect their national character, while accepting change and opening their minds to the influences of the world.

"Nationalism can serve as a stepping-stone toward international understanding. Is it not our childhood familiarity with the fields and the forests around our house which enables us to move with

8

assurance on the soil of others? Is it not on the basis of an insight into our mother tongue that we learn to speak other languages more easily?

"The United Nations is an expression of our will to find a synthesis between the nation and the world. It is an attempt to provide us with a framework inside which it is possible to serve the world by serving our nations, and to serve our nations by serving the world.

"What is in the national interest, when truly seen, merges naturally into the international interest."

❡ Men organize themselves into families. The families join together in villages or tribes. The tribes and the villages fuse into peoples, and one day, out of the self-consciousness of a people, there develops a feeling of difference and separateness, the positive expression of which is a feeling of nationhood. The nation organizes its life within a set of constitutional rules, evolving in practice or crystallized as law. Under the constitution the people develop national organs with different functions and a division of responsibilities representing a balance of power. Through those organs laws are given, setting the pattern for the lives and activities of the individuals and the groups which constitute the nation.

Is that the end of the road of the development of human society? Of course not. Nation borders on nation, peoples get in touch with each other, and whatever differences there may exist and whatever conflicts of interest the people may see, they are forced to live together, fighting or in peace, as neighbors with limits put by nature to their possible self-sufficiency and for that reason with a need to develop forms for international intercourse, permitting more or less highly developed degrees of cooperation. So an institutional system of coexistence is developed with its rules and practices. Still there is no international society. Still the nation remains the highest full organized form for the life of peoples.

However primitive a basic institutional pattern may be, it

carries within it seeds for the growth of higher social organisms, covering wider areas and groups of peoples. [9]

❨ Everybody today, with part of his being, belongs to one country, with its specific traditions and problems, while with another part he has become a citizen of a world which no longer permits national isolation. Seen in this light there could not be any conflict between nationalism and internationalism, between the nation and the world. [27]

❨ None of us can make ourselves entirely free from our own background, and why should we? Is not the national accent and the national experience very often a great asset in international cooperation? [22]

❨ This nationalism can be a constructive element, raising the dignity and stature of peoples and mobilizing their best moral resources. But, in a period of severe emotional strains, it may also find expressions which are in fact hostile to the steady growth of the very national life it aims to serve. The United Nations may help in avoiding such a self-defeating development. [32]

❨ ... It appears evident that no nation or group of nations can base its future on a claim of supremacy. It is in its own interest that the other groups have opportunities equal to those it has had itself. To contribute to this is an act of solidarity which is not only good for the whole, but, in the long run, redounds to the advantage even of those who take action. It means that leadership is substituted for power—leadership both in giving other peoples their chances and in assisting them, without issuing commands, to find the best way to develop their spiritual and material resources.

Political independence, whether in a developed country or underdeveloped country, can exist and thrive only in a society of nations in which national and international interests harmonize. [16]

⟨ When you speak and act for national policies that will strengthen the influence of the United Nations you are doing so because you believe that this is best for your country as well as for humanity. [23]

⟨ We often see the word "nationalism" used in a derogatory sense. The same is true of the word "internationalism." When nationalism connotes, for example, a "go-it-alone" isolationism, and internationalism an outlook which belittles the significance of national life and of nations as centers of political action and spiritual tradition, the words become contradictory and the attitudes they describe irreconcilable. [27]

⟨ . . . We get in a first, necessarily rudimentary form, a form of society which, while preserving and protecting the lives of the nations, points toward an international constitutional system surmounting the nations, utilizing them to the extent that smaller units are more efficient instruments for evolution, but creating rules which limit the influence of the nations in fields where bigger units present greater possibilities for development and survival. [9]

⟨ The United Nations exists because a shrinking world, in which no nation or group of nations can live any more unto itself alone, has made world organization necessary for the purposes expressed in the Charter. Enlightened national policies, constructive bilateral and regional arrangements—political and economic—all have an essential place in contributing toward greater security from war and in promoting economic and social progress, provided they are pursued as parts of a greater whole in which the interdependence of all regions of the world is recognized. [76]

⟨ There is a new situation the day you have to recognize that you cannot dictate to other nations and that you are not independent of the actions of other nations. Looking back into the past we see how peoples have been oppressed—and how peoples have accepted oppression—in the name of God. May we not be approaching a time when in His name they will instead be giving and accepting freedom? [27]

❨ The Charter lay down some basic rules of international ethics by which all member states have committed themselves to be guided. To a large extent, the rules reflect standards accepted as binding for life within states. Thus, they appear, in the main, as a projection into the international arena and the international community of purposes and principles already accepted as being of national validity.

. . . Due to different traditions, the state of social development and the character of national institutions, wide variations naturally exist as to the application in national life of the principles reflected in the Charter, but it is not too difficult to recognize the common elements behind those differences. It is therefore not surprising that such principles of national application could be transposed into an agreed basis also for international behavior and cooperation. [19]

❨ Systems of alliance, maintained side by side with the United Nations in recognition of the prevailing balance of forces, may serve a useful purpose during the period through which we are passing. However, most of us agree that such systems of alliance, like other traditional means of diplomacy and defense of the national interest, are limited in their value as safeguards of the present and future security and welfare of our countries. Nations and groups of nations will never again be able to live and to arrogate judgment unto themselves in international affairs in ways which once were a matter of course. [38]

❨ There is a price to be paid for organized international cooperation. But it is a far lesser price than the one that would be exacted from any nation that attempted in this day and generation to "go it alone." [23]

3

Universality

The word "universality" does not appear in the United Nations Charter in reference to membership. Universal membership is in fact hampered by the use of the word "peaceloving." Since the United Nations is composed of "peaceloving" nations, any nation which in the opinion of the majority does not love peace enough can be excluded. For this reason, and for others, one quarter of humankind is not represented in the World Organization.

Hammarskjöld felt that the concept of universality was nevertheless implicit in the logic of the Charter and the only possible basis for an ideal Organization. "I want the whole of mankind represented in the United Nations because it is a platform where all people should have the opportunity of speaking for themselves."

Lack of universality, he thought, was one of the main weaknesses of the League of Nations, which after the United States had rejected it became a sort of holy alliance of nations still imbued with nineteenth-century ideas. This germ of exclusiveness was then carried over to the United Nations. But, said Hammarskjöld, surely it is much better to have a country inside the Organization than outside it, because having it outside means that one is denied certain ways of thrashing out difficulties. "Whatever your views and whatever your differences with others," he told a press conference in Canberra in 1956, "it is much better to have . . . contact and negotiation available than not to have it available."

He recognized that universality would increase not only the potentialities of the Organization, but also its difficulties. However, no difficulty would have seemed so tragic to him as the fact that today, owing to the absence of Communist China and other participants in the Vietnam conflict, this war cannot be fought at the Security Council table.

❲ The League [of Nations] represented a stage in political development where the preponderance of the West, of Europe, was very strong indeed. . . . There was not even a semblance of universality in the modern sense of the word, although there was a kind of universality in the classical sense of the word, with Western predominance. That was inherent weakness, which I feel, looking backward, was bound to break the back of the first experiment. [3]

❲ It has so often been said that the world of today is one which requires organized international cooperation on a basis of universality that one repeats it with hesitation. . . . No international policy for the future can be envisaged which does not recognize this principle and is not willing to give it adequate implementation in practice.

Were it to be felt that the Organization with its present procedures failed to provide the best means by which this basic principle could now be implemented, we would be facing a situation where the choice would be one between revolution and evolution. We should have to choose between the creation of a new international organization, based on the principle of universality like the United Nations, although different in other respects, and an evolution of procedures of the present Organization which would make it a more adequate instrument for implementation of the principle. [17]

❲ I believe that the United Nations is a "must" in view of the problem before us. We need a universal organization, and for that reason the Organization in which we work has to be universal. In that sense, you may say that it is the one—I would not call it hope—method by which we can approach the world peace problem from this angle. [48]

❲ It seems to me that the idea of the United Nations as a club to which only the like-minded will be admitted, in which membership is a privilege and expulsion is the retribution for wrongdoing, is totally unrealistic and self-defeating. [23]

❲ So long as the United Nations continues to fall so far short of universality of membership, it is true that there will remain serious obstacles to its effective use in some questions of world concern. [78]

4

Peace and Human Rights

That all human beings have the same rights simply by the fact of being born is a conception old in the law of God, but it has been slow to find acceptance in the laws of man, and the process is far from complete. The Second World War was an agonizing offense against humanity, and the United Nations Charter takes note of it in requiring of its members respect for observance of human rights and fundamental freedom for all "without distinction as to race, sex, language, or religion."

Broadly defined, fundamental freedom means the right to security: that is, the individual's right to free development within the limits set by the right of others to the same. Security cannot flourish in an atmosphere of fear, and Hammarskjöld correctly saw that individual rights were closely linked with the issue of war and peace. "Without recognition of human rights, we shall never have peace; and it is only within the framework of peace that human rights can be fully developed. In fact, the work for peace is basically a work for the most elementary human right: the right of everyone to security and freedom from fear."

The United Nations has no right to lay down a law within a nation. It cannot protect any group of people from persecution or from any infringement of their rights. It can only embody the spirit of the Charter and define the goals which, as Hammarskjöld said, "should be the laws of the future in each nation."

The Universal Declaration of Human Rights is a step in the proper direction. It lays forth a standard of conduct for governments toward the governed and for the governed toward each other. While not part of the Charter, it grew out of it and was appoved by the General Assembly on December 10, 1948.

❲ The development of social justice is closely connected with the problem of human rights. Such international legal instruments as the proposed covenants on human rights are parts of a concerted effort that is in fact proceeding on a much wider basis. Fundamentally, the rate of progress will be determined by the degree to which the developing social conscience of the peoples of the world is able to find expression not only in national legislation and in international treaties, but in the climate of opinion in the various regions of the world. The Universal Declaration of Human Rights should set a standard for achievement that will guide opinion in this field, which is so essential to the ultimate success of the United Nations. [76]

❲ The Universal Declaration is not, of course, a treaty and has, in itself, no force in law. But, as "a common standard of achievement for all peoples and all nations," it not only crystallizes the political thought of our times on these matters, but it has also influenced the thinking of legislators all over the world.

The relationship of man to society is a relationship for which every generation must seek to find the proper form. But, just as ideas far back in the past gave direction to the efforts for the best in former times, so this declaration should give direction to those who now carry the responsibility for a sound development of society.

It is also, in words for our time, a reminder of what must be the goal for the individual as well as for governments; the recognition in action of the dignity of man and of the sanctity of those freedoms which follow from such recognition.

Why is war and fear of war in the headlines of every daily paper, if not because man fears man and nation nation? Could there be a more eloquent sign of how far we are from recognition of the philosophy behind the principles of human rights on which alone peace can be built? Can there be a greater challenge for us to work for such a recognition of the dignity of man as would eliminate the fear which is eating our world like a cancer?

What is the right of freedom from attack? Is it not the right to freedom from fear?

Thus we see how close the links are between the philosophy reflected in the recognition of the rights of individuals and the basic principles which may decide the issue of war and peace.

If, at long last, the recognition of human dignity means to give others freedom from fear, then that recognition cannot be simply a question of passive acceptance. It is a question of the positive action that must be taken in order to kill fear. [30]

❲ International instruments embodying the principles contained in the Universal Declaration of Human Rights do not yet appear to meet with general acceptance. . . .

It should not be surprising that, having laid down universal standards in an area where cultural differences are so wide and fundamental, the United Nations should experience some difficulties in finding practical methods to enhance the adoption and implementation of these standards on a world-wide basis. These inevitable difficulties should not generate a sense of frustration, nor should they prompt the Organization to actions with doubtful implications. In carrying out its obligations under the Charter in the field of human rights, the Organization should favor initiatives leading forward without introducing the risk of sterile and endless controversy. [78]

❨ Human Rights—their counterpart is human obligations. In celebrating Human Rights Day we should remember that no declarations on human rights, nor even any conventions or laws protecting human rights, are sufficient for their purpose unless we recognize, as a personal responsibility, respect in word and deed for the dignity of the human being.

A great German philosopher formulated the underlying principle when he said that the basic rule of ethics is never to treat man as a means but always as an end. In less paradoxical forms the same thought is common to all the great religions represented in this Organization. And yet, we witness daily actions which may slip through the network of general statements and of law, but yet brutally reflect man's cruelty to man, and men's abuse of men. We witness it on a national level and we witness it on the international level. [73]

❨ With respect to the United Nations as a symbol of faith, it may in this perspective be said that to very many it stands as a kind of "yes" to the ability of man to form his own destiny, and form his own destiny so as to create a world where the dignity of man can come fully into its own. [8]

5

Disarmament

The chief dilemma of our age, as Hammarskjöld saw it, stems from a deadlock that has occurred in our thinking: the notion that national security must depend upon military supremacy. Thus we find it impossible to grow out of a world of armaments into a world of security based on international law. He exhorted the powers to break this deadlock. "What is of the utmost importance . . . and urgency," he told both Houses of Parliament in London in 1958, "is . . . to win agreement upon some first step or steps which would put some brake upon the armaments race."

Like a good mountaineer, he had respect for tiny steps; in fact, he did not believe in broad, sweeping, propaganda-minded statements where disarmament was concerned. He wanted concrete agreements, small, but possible, which could be integrated into a far-reaching plan extending toward the ideal target: total disarmament. The main obstacle was what Martin Buber called "existential mistrust," when man, instead of looking for intercourse with his fellow man, tries to "see through and unmask him." When such attitudes become imbued—and they do become imbued, especially in diplomatic life—then, said Hammarskjöld, we risk that "speech turns into dumbness and sense into madness."

There is only one possible solution: controlled disarmament; and this was possible, in Hammarskjöld's view, only through the

United Nations. Any disarmament system has to be administered by a World Organization whose members include almost all the nations of the world.

"Some say, 'What is the use of discussing disarmament? If the political situation improves, disarmament will follow.'

"They overlook one essential factor: that the very study of disarmament," just in sounding each other out, "may be the vehicle for progress toward greater . . . understanding."

⟪ The science of total war, the steady progress of which we have witnessed during this century, has proceeded, through the organization of greater and greater mass armies and more and more deadly weapons, to its present climax of destructiveness. In the event of another world war, each side now faces the almost certain prospect of receiving mortal wounds. This adds a new dimension to the problems of collective security and disarmament. As the meaning of the new situation in which we find ourselves becomes clearer, I trust that new approaches to those problems will be opened before us where now there seems to be only a blank wall. [77]

⟪ It seems unrealistic to approach the total problem oblivious of the fact that all political experience and all previous negotiation show that the road to progress lies in the direction of efforts to contain and reduce the area of disagreement by mobilizing such common interests as may exist and as may override other and special interests tending in the opposite direction. [18]

⟪ A very limited number of countries hold key positions in the field of armaments, so that any effort on a universal basis and by voting, to reach a decision having practical force, would be ineffective, unless founded on a basic agreement between those few parties mostly concerned. Therefore, direct negotiations between those countries are an essential first step to the solution, through the United Nations, of the disarmament problem, and do not in any way derogate from the responsibilities or rights of the Organization. [19]

⟪ The actual establishment of an agreed international system for the control and reduction of armaments and armed forces can take place only in an atmosphere of confidence, trust, and understanding among the nations, an atmosphere which has not yet come into being. But it was a mistake to draw from this the conclusion, as some did, that there was no use in the meantime striving for such agreement. The exchange of views, the explorations of the respective positions, that have been taking place in the Disarmament Sub-Committee and in the General Assembly have been an essential part of the processes through which the Member Governments have sought to find their way in their search for increased understanding and confidence. [78]

⟪ It seems to me that statements made from various quarters indicate a few changes in the approach. One is that there is a greater willingness to consider, let us say, partial solutions. Previously, it has always been a question of some kind of total solution. I do not believe in that kind of package deal. I do not think that that ever works out in a situation so complicated as this one. So we must get to the stage where it is a recognized possibility to approach it pragmatically and step by step. [65]

⟪ There can be no solution to the disarmament problem short of the acceptance of total disarmament under satisfactory control by both sides. The pragmatic approach and the, so to say, global one are not at variance, for it is obvious that efforts to avoid a widening of the field of conflict and to reduce the area in which concrete agreement for the moment is impossible should at all events be integrated into a wider, more far-reaching plan under which the security interests of the parties can be balanced out against each other in ways that will make it possible for the parties to reach the ideal target of total disarmament. [18]

❲ The other day I read a book by Arthur Waley, one of the great interpreters of Chinese thought and literature and one of those great Jewish students of humane letters who have so splendidly enriched our cultural tradition. In his work Waley quotes what an early Chinese historian had to say about the philosopher Sung Tzu and his followers, some 350 years B.C. To one who works in the United Nations, the quotation strikes a familiar note. It runs as follows:

> *Constantly rebuffed but never discouraged, they went around from State to State helping people to settle their differences, arguing against wanton attack and pleading for the suppression of arms, that the age in which they lived might be saved from its state of continual war. To this end they interviewed princes and lectured the common people, nowhere meeting with any great success, but obstinately persisting in their task, till kings and commoners alike grew weary of listening to them. Yet undeterred they continued to force themselves on people's attention.*

Is this a description of a quixotic group, whose efforts are doomed to failure? The wording, with its tone of frustration, may lead us to think so. However, I believe that this interpretation would be wrong. The historian tells us about a group engaged in a struggle he considers very much worth while and one which will have to go on until success is achieved. [34]

❲ It is when we all play safe that we create a world of the utmost insecurity. [30]

6

Atomic Nightmare

Hammarskjöld's nightmares proved to be, on occasion, profoundly irritating to the great powers. When the Soviet Union announced its decision unilaterally to suspend atomic testing, the United States saw in it nothing but a propaganda move and severely reprimanded the Secretary-General for publicly expressing his satisfaction. Similarly, when he hailed the United States proposal to establish an Arctic inspection zone as a safeguard against surprise attack, the Soviet Union rebuffed him.

To both powers he spoke gravely of the "crisis of trust" brought about by the Cold War. He refused to be silenced on the touchy subject. He saw it as his right to intervene in support of the Charter's purposes, and his duty toward nations menaced by nuclear destruction to act as their spokesman.

"We have a long road ahead of us to traverse before we can hope to eliminate the threat. . . . But we cannot hope to travel at all unless we begin to take down the barriers to understanding and friendship and begin to work together in growing confidence."

Negotiations between the nuclear powers for the suspension of tests were begun in his lifetime and these led to an agreement after his death.

❨ The stalemate in the field of disarmament has been permitted to last for far too long. Attempts to break it through negotiations have so far proved of no avail. I think there are reasons of different kinds behind this deeply worrying failure. One is that in a sense governments have been too ambitious, not being satisfied with just making a dent in this intricate and vital problem from which a rift could develop, opening up the possibilities of a true exchange of views. Another reason has been the tendency for each government to wait for others to take the first step. Still another reason and, of course, the basic one, is the crisis of trust from which all mankind is suffering at the present juncture and which is reflected in an unwillingness to take any moves in a positive direction at their face value and a tendency to hold back a positive response because of a fear of being misled.

I have felt it incumbent on me to state these few simple reactions. I have done so under my obligations to the peoples whose voice is reflected in the Charter under which I am acting. I trust that my intervention will not be misinterpreted as a taking of sides, but merely as an expression of profound feelings which are current all over the world and which have a right to be heard here also outside the framework of government policies.

I hope that each one of the governments represented around this table will wish to try out the line of trust as a way out of the disintegration and decline under which we all now suffer.

Each government is in close contact with the opinion of the man in the street in its own country. For that reason, I am sure that all governments are in a position to confirm my statement that the peoples are eagerly and anxiously expecting leadership bringing them out of the present nightmare. The government taking a fruitful initiative will be hailed as a benefactor by the peoples. The governments responding in a positive spirit so as to give effect to such an attempt to turn the development will share the merit with the one who took the first step.

You know that I have expressed myself many times in press conferences on disarmament. It is, of course, an extremely complicated problem and it is bound to develop slowly. But there is a point in the development of disarmament where every time an initiative is taken in good faith and its possible consequences, its possible values, are not fully explored, I have the feeling that we have missed the bus. And we should not be too sure that the road will remain open for buses in all the future. That sense of urgency, that sense of responsibility, in the face of every new opening, from wherever it comes and whatever its immediate limited substance, was what prompted me, what made me feel that it was one of those occasions where public statements by the Secretary-General are very much part of his duty and a very adequate supplement to private diplomacy.

It is all right to continue disarmament talks if it is just a high political game or some kind of refined chess, or something else, provided nothing develops in the meantime. But if, in the meantime, the armaments race continues up to a point where it does represent a risk of failure, of breakdown, of collisions which are unintentional, then, of course, an element of urgency is introduced which makes it impossible to look with equanimity at the diplomatic game.

I do not believe that any of the governments concerned have less of a sense of urgency than I have. But it may be that the way in which discussion has been pursued has tended to mislead public opinion so that they have felt: "Well, this is in the hands of the governments, and they talk and write letters and discuss matters and meet, and we can go on in the shadow of that somewhat costly but not harmful operation."

The people who give thoughtful consideration to the news know that there is a margin of failure everywhere in everything and that there is a factor of impatience. They might rightly feel that it is not in keeping with their reasonable rights to life to have to live under the kind of threat which is created not by any specific policy of any country but which emerges from the total situation as it develops while the discussions are going on. [42]

7

The Atom for Peace

Hammarskjöld was not a master of dramatic phrases and pathetic outbursts. His speeches were calm and measured, and they bore the mark of optimism. But once, talking of the arms race, disarmament, and the possibility of atomic destruction, he permitted himself to use the word "nightmare."

"The kind of language I rarely use," he said later. "However, it was completely adequate for me as a description of what I had in mind."

In the forefront of Hammarskjöld's thinking was the awareness that with the harnessing of nuclear energy man stands at the crossroads of plenty or of extermination, and he greeted not only with words but with action every manifestation by the atomic powers that they were on the side of the angels. After President Eisenhower's Atoms for Peace proposal to the General Assembly on December 8, 1953, Hammarskjöld organized, with the help of a Scientific Advisory Committee, two international scientific conferences, in 1955 and 1958, in which thousands of scientists and engineers from both sides of the Iron Curtain took part.

Hammarskjöld hoped that such nonpolitical gatherings might ease tensions and turn minds from war to peace. Indeed, as a result of the first conference, the International Atomic Energy Agency, which works for the peaceful uses of nuclear energy, was established in Vienna.

❡ The great scientific discoveries in the atomic field have, as you well know, given entirely new dimensions to the problem of armaments and war. At the same time they have opened vistas to a new age of plenty, following a new industrial revolution. In both respects the world community is faced with a major challenge which cannot be solved within the limited orbit of any single nation.

The first Geneva Conference paved the way . . . for the creation of the new Atomic Agency, which after long negotiations was set up last year in Vienna. In both respects the United Nations proved to be a valuable instrument of negotiation and bridge building. Without the United Nations, this creative process, assuming it would have been possible at all, would undoubtedly have taken much longer and been much more complicated. [12]

❡ The atmosphere of fear and suspicion should not be permitted to prevent a constructive approach to international partnership in the development of atomic energy for peaceful purposes. [78]

❡ Put to peaceful uses, atomic energy offers hitherto undreamed-of opportunities, especially for that vast majority of humanity that is still living in poverty in the economically underdeveloped areas of the world. If the atmosphere of fear and suspicion were to bar us from a constructive approach to these opportunities, thus leaving atomic energy merely as a basis for further destruction, we would have to register a new and probably fatal failure, for we would thus not only maintain present tensions but cultivate the soil for new tensions leading to new wars. [77]

❡ Our world of today . . . required a universal vision—indeed, our anguished hearts demanded it. Mankind as an ideal was not too weak a guide for our conduct. It was necessary, more necessary than ever, to seek in it an inspiration for all our actions. [27]

8

Outer Space

"Ironically enough, as a by-product of war effort we see the beginning of a penetration into outer space with all the possibilities for new progress and new difficulties which this entails."

Hammarskjöld was determined that earthly difficulties should remain on earth and not be extended into the firmament. There exists in fact a tacit acceptance among nations that outer space—as distinct from air space—belongs to no one and cannot be appropriated by any nation. In order to ensure that this happy situation should continue, Hammarskjöld encouraged international negotiation. He wanted the General Assembly to agree on a basic rule regulating the use of outer space and celestial bodies, and he favored the establishment of international machinery to foster cooperation.

"It is for man to decide," he said, "whether outer space will be a new source of prosperity or a new source of holocaust."

❡ We have here a vital field of activities and joint interests for which rules must be established and procedures must be created that will render it possible for the world community to safeguard the observance of those rules. A new need for international negotiations and for the establishment of appropriate international organs has thus come into being.

It would be my hope that the General Assembly, as a result of its consideration, would find the way to an agreement on a basic rule that outer space, and the celestial bodies therein, are not considered as capable of appropriation by any state, and that it would further affirm the overriding interest of the community of nations in the peaceful and beneficial use of outer space and initiate steps for an international machinery to further this end. [12]

❨ Warning words about how the development of social organization, and how the growth of moral maturity in the emerging mass civilizations, has lagged behind the technical and scientific progress have been repeated so often as to sound hackneyed—and to make us forget that they are true. [11]

9

Science and Holocaust

Hammarskjöld, with his taste for abstractions, saw in science that symbol of universality which always touched him to express anew his belief in the brotherhood of man. He was in his element talking to scientists, whom he compared favorably with the garden variety of politicians, for they were not concerned with expediency, strategy, or tactics, but with "the search for truth." They would expiate on behalf of all of us our feeling of guilt that in our folly we have thought of no better use for a great discovery than to manufacture deadly instruments of annihilation.

In a speech at the Rockefeller Institute in 1960, he quoted some opinions of the atomic scientist Dr. J. Robert Oppenheimer: "Science profits by bringing two sets of techniques or ideas into touch with one another. The sciences fertilize each other; they grow by contact and common enterprise."

Hammarskjöld extended these ideas, saying that they were true not only about science, but of all those activities which create human society. He wanted all such interests brought together within the sphere of the United Nations. Organized coexistence was his idea, with the United Nations as a nexus, and he never ceased to hammer home the prerequisite: a recognition of the fundamental unity of all mankind, of its interest in peace and in progress based on justice and freedom.

❰ Scientists of genius, working . . . in . . . research centers around the world, have made a unique contribution to progress, prosperity, and peace. If their achievements have been turned to uses sometimes very far from their original intentions, it is not their fault. Nor is it the fault of their colleagues in the fields of theology, law, medicine, history, and philosophy, or other branches of humane letters, if their contributions have not sufficed to create such psychological and political safeguards as would guarantee that the achievements of science be turned to man's benefit and not to his destruction. [11]

❰ The discoveries and inventions which have opened the doors for personal contacts all around the globe, and for the written and spoken word in every quarter, have, at the same time, put at our disposal means by which we have unprecedented possibilities to change conditions of life for the better, for all people. Our increased knowledge has given us new sources of power and new insight into the nature of disease. It may be that we are still far from mastering disease, and it may be that we are still far from mastering the new sources of energy sufficiently well to meet the demand of a quickly growing humanity for a life of dignity without fear. But, the newly developed perspectives are such that political economy need no longer be the "dismal science" of the days of Malthus.

If the United Nations is to succeed in giving to the development of the world all that . . . organized coexistence can yield, it will be on the basis of a recognition of our fundamental unity . . . and through the devoted efforts of men, who . . . dare to be pioneers in their field of activity and who dare to risk "a fruitful mistake" in their effort to meet the challenges of an ever-widening knowledge and of ever-widening—but also ever more complex— human relationships.

Our world of change is one in which only those who show this intellectual and moral courage—and who are free to exercise it—will be able to face the challenge of the future.

One risk, facing equally the worker, the artist, the scientist, and the politician, is the suppression of the inner freedom of the individual through demands for subordination and conformity. There is less tolerance for the personal, perhaps erratic, experiment in life than in times which could afford more tolerance. However, the need for such tolerance is as great as ever in the very interest of progress and in the interest of peace.

In very simple words, one of the leading nuclear physicists [J. Robert Oppenheimer] has formulated our personal problem when he says that the ways that we learned in our childhood are now only very meagerly adequate for the issues that we must meet in maturity. His words stress how developing knowledge and technology, and a developing society, require of us a continuous development also of the individual. [43]

(Science and technology have given mankind new power to destroy itself. But together with this, we know that the opportunity for economic and social progress for all men now lies within our power to an extent that previous generations have not known. [76]

Public Diplomacy

Before the First World War the conversations of diplomats were conducted behind closed doors in gilded chancelleries and were not considered to be the business of the public whose welfare depended upon them. Woodrow Wilson brought about a partial change with his doctrine of "open covenants, openly arrived at." The League of Nations deliberated in public, inaugurating something that was later to be called "conference diplomacy." Still, many important and fateful discussions were held in secret.

In our time, when the fate of the many depends on the outcome of negotiations among the few, we have "multilateral diplomacy," which is, as Dag Hammarskjöld said, "by its very nature such that secrecy has lost its place and justification." Today's diplomat must have public opinion behind him, he must feel the deep and decisive aspirations that live in the minds of the people. No government and no statesman can go "against prevailing public opinion or lead in a direction the public is not prepared to follow."

The United Nations lives in a glass house, and in Hammarskjöld's view "it should operate in a glass house in order to serve its purpose."

❪ It is part of the diplomat's responsibility not only to lead public opinion toward acceptance of the lasting consequences of the interdependence of our world. He must also help public opinion to become as accustomed to the necessity for give and take and for compromise in international politics as it has long been on questions of state and local concern.

No diplomat is likely to meet the demands of public opinion on him as a representative in international policy unless he understands this opinion and unless he respects it deeply enough to give it leadership when he feels that the opinion does not truly represent the deeper and finally decisive aspirations in the minds and hearts of the people.

Least tangible, but perhaps most important new factor in diplomacy: mass public opinion as a living force in international affairs. Of course, this public opinion has as its background the new mass media of communication, but as a psychological phenomenon and a political factor it is not sufficiently explained by this background. It is the expression of a democratic mass civilization that is still in its infancy, giving to the man in the street and to group reactions a new significance in foreign policy.

In the modern world of mass media and publicity no diplomat trying to respond to the demands of the situations can be only a servant. He must to some extent and in some respects also be a leader by looking beyond the immediate future and going underneath the superficial reactions, be they expressed by powerful news organs catering to what they believe to be the wishes of the broad masses—wishes which may in reality be as loosely attached to the man in the street as the suits which he decides to wear this year.

The dipomat may still confer behind closed doors, but he will be met by reporters and photographers when he comes out. His words will reach everybody by press and film and radio and television. His personality will be known to vast numbers for whom in other times he would have been only a name, or less than a name.

No diplomat can depart too far from what is accepted or acceptable to public opinion in those quarters which give weight to his arguments. But it does not follow from this that he should simply let himself be guided by anticipated reactions of the public.

A first and major change in diplomatic techniques that is called for by development is the introduction of what might be described as the multilateral element. I do not mean to suggest that bilateral diplomatic contacts and negotiations have lost their old importance, only that they prove insufficient. In a world of interdependence means must be devised for a broadening of the approach so that the interests of a group of nations or of the community of nations are given their necessary weight.

The diplomat who works bilaterally on a national basis without the widest perspective, without recognition—and a proper handling—of the publicity aspect of his work, or without giving to public opinion its proper place in the picture, has little place in our world of today. [24]

⟨ I think that the days of the classical French diplomacy are over. I would almost say that I think that the old technique is a good one, the old technique which required a reasonable degree of quiet about what was being done, a reasonable degree of tact and responsibility. But there is a new element in the picture, and that new element you might, if you like, call the American one, as [Harold] Nicholson does, and that is an element of frankness and directness; and it is quite easy to combine that with discretion and quiet. [69]

❡ . . . The transition to public diplomacy allows public opinion to follow the unfolding of diplomatic operations and, conversely, it offers an opportunity for public opinion to influence the position taken in the course of the negotiations. [6]

❡ . . . Experience so far with respect to the work of the General Assembly points out what everybody recognizes as the greatest danger and perhaps the greatest weakness. It is that everything is enacted in the glaring light of publicity. I say "glaring" because every gesture, every shift of expression of the face and every change of the voice are enlarged and given back to the public of the world and, for that reason, are over-simplified. In the transition from thinking to speaking, something may be lost. In the transition from public speaking to the headlines of the papers of the world, very much is lost. [8]

❡ It is impossible to negotiate without a reasonable degree of secrecy, but I think that on the other hand you should maintain as much publicity as you can, that is, all the publicity that does not interfere with the proper development of your arguments, the testing out of your grounds, and all that. I can well understand the old view that what you do behind closed doors is likely to be something which you want to keep secret. I think that the good modern diplomat does not want the results of what he is doing to be kept secret at all. On the contrary, he wants to bring it home to the public, but he asks for the quiet necessary in order to achieve the maximum of results. [69]

❡ The ultimate test of a diplomacy adequate to our world is its capacity to evoke this kind of response from the people and thus to rally public opinion behind what is wise and necessary for the peace and progress of the world. [24]

⟨ The value of public diplomacy in the United Nations will depend to a decisive extent on how far the responsible spokesmen find it possible to rise above a narrow tactical approach to the politics of international life, and to speak as men for aspirations and hopes which are those of *all* mankind. [12]

11

Quiet Diplomacy

While holding the view that matters of great moment should be threshed out in full view of the public and in harmony with their wishes, Hammarskjöld nevertheless recognized certain inevitable practical drawbacks to total openness in diplomacy. It might happen, for example, that a delegate to the United Nations, finding himself in the full glare of the television cameras, might rise to the occasion by making propaganda points for the edification of the people back home; or he might "play to the gallery." Once he has taken such a public stance, however impracticable, it is hard for him to retreat from it.

In national parliaments, we are used to public debate. Our party might win or lose, but we accept the fact that both winners and losers must in the long run work out a compromise. International diplomacy has not yet reached that state of maturity. Concessions made in public may be taken for weakness or appeasement; they may cause a country to "lose face." Open diplomacy therefore risks becoming frozen diplomacy, in which compromise is impossible.

Hammarskjöld therefore advocated a balance between public diplomacy and what he called "quiet" diplomacy. His personal gift of persuasiveness and what some people thought of as his "compelling integrity" could be called successfully into play in private conversations where political differences are diluted and "the human factor carries more weight . . . and confidential exchanges are possible even across frontiers which otherwise appear impossible."

He was frequently criticized for these quiet habits, but he told the press: *"It is more important to achieve* de facto *successes, even if they are unknown to the public, than to endanger a* de facto *success because of too great a willingness to sell the United Nations."*

Speaking before the Houses of Parliament in London in 1958 he said, *"Long experience has shown that negotiation in public alone does not produce results. If the United Nations is to serve as an increasingly effective instrument of negotiation, the principles and methods of traditional diplomacy need to be applied more fully alongside its public procedures."*

❲ I would not for a moment suggest that the functions of debate and vote do not have their essential place in world affairs today. Nor would I suggest that any step be taken that would retard the development of an increasingly influential role for a well-informed public opinion in the making of foreign policy. But the United Nations is subject to the same principles as apply to diplomacy in all its forms. [13]

❲ The Organization should be more than an instrument of what may be described as conference diplomacy. This new diplomacy, with its public debates, serves and will continue to serve many essential needs in the international life of our times. It is not, however, sufficient for the efforts towards understanding and reconciliation which are of such importance now. The United Nations can and should support these efforts in other ways. Conference diplomacy may usefully be supplemented by more quiet diplomacy within the United Nations, whether directly between representatives of Member Governments or in contacts between the Secretary-General and Member Governments. [78]

❨ The United Nations is not an instrument for so-called appease-ment from the point of view of either side, but it is a platform where a business-like mutual exploration can go beyond what is possible in regular diplomatic forms. The public diplomacy of United Nations meetings, and the private diplomacy for which the United Nations also provides a framework, have served and will continue to serve to limit and reduce the impact of the basic conflicts. [12]

❨ You can only hope to find a lasting solution to a conflict if you have learned to see the other objectively, but, at the same time, to experience his difficulties subjectively. [83]

❨ COOKE: Wilson's remark about "open covenants, openly arrived at." But in point of fact that did not happen, did it?

HAMMARSKJÖLD: No, it did not.

COOKE: Would you agree with Sir Anthony Eden who several months ago said he believed in the Wilsonian concept, as he said with a slight emendation: "I believe in open covenants, secretly arrived at." Is that fair enough?

H: It is a very good slogan, really a very brilliant way of re-writing the Wilson statement. It's fair enough, but I would like to qualify it: secretly arrived at, yes; quietly arrived at to the extent that such quiet is necessary. [69]

❨ The road toward more satisfactory forms of organization for a world community of states does not lead through publicized "successes" of the United Nations. It leads through a series of good or bad experiences with the specific techniques made pos-sible by the United Nations. It goes via the conclusions we are able to draw, in action, about these experiences. In this respect, the continuous, but unsensational and therefore little-known, work on current tasks which is conducted within the United Nations is also of importance. [6]

⟨ Over the years, the diplomatic representatives accredited to the United Nations have developed a cooperation and built mutual contacts in dealing with problems they have in common, which in reality make them members of a kind of continuous diplomatic conference, in which they are informally following and able to discuss, on a personal basis, all political questions which are important for the work of the Organization. These continuous informal deliberations do not lend themselves to publicity, and they receive none. But it would be a grave mistake to conclude from this that they are unimportant. [10]

⟨ The most dangerous of all moral dilemmas: when we are obliged to conceal truth in order to help the truth to be victorious. If this should at any time become our duty in the role assigned us by fate, how straight must be our path at all times if we are not to perish. [83]

⟨ The independent opinion which gives the negotiations in the United Nations their special character is formed as much outside the conference halls as inside them. [10]

⟨ There is so much that happens at dinner parties in all sorts of ways, and you always have an element of quiet diplomacy, whether it is recognized or not.

You know that general notion that a diplomat is some chap in a homburg and striped pants, that is widespread. And I regret it, because it certainly adds to the difficulties of all of us in this curious profession. We are just like anybody else, only some with peculiar tasks, that's all. Any man of common sense, clean, can play that game. There is nothing so peculiar in a diplomat. [69]

12

United Nations Diplomacy

Diplomacy must surely be one of the oldest professions. One cannot imagine a man or group of men who have no need to negotiate; and it is very likely that cavemen and the emissaries of Egypt or Greece had to approach their problem of communication in much the same way as the ambassadors of the nineteenth century.

Today the hydrogen bomb has revolutionized the technique of warfare, and its dire consequences—the destruction of vast areas, the death of millions, and economic ruin lasting over long periods of time—has made war the concern of all. A new interdependence among nations has come about.

Hammarskjöld admonished that old-fashioned diplomatic dialogue was no longer possible. It is for this very reason that we need the United Nations, a place of "multi-laterial diplomatic contact," of confabulations open to all interested parties. The fate not of nations but of communities of nations is at stake. The atom-age ambassador speaks not only in the interests of his own country, but also shares the responsibility for other nations represented around the conference table. The negotiations do not stop at the conference room but continue outside it in offices, hotel rooms, and even at social gatherings. The United Nations has become in reality a continuous diplomatic conference, partly open and partly private. The installation of the new diplomatic

*corps in permanent delegations around the United Nations Plaza
enables the Secretary-General to carry on frequent consultations
on a high level.*

(In the General Assembly, as well as in the Councils, open
debate is the rule. The public and the press are admitted to
practically all meetings and are able to follow the development
of arguments, the evolution of conflicts, and the arrival at solutions. The debates cover a ground which in earlier times was
mostly reserved for negotiation behind closed doors. They have
introduced a new instrument of negotiation, that of conference
diplomacy. This instrument has many advantages. It can serve
to form public opinion. It can subject national policies and
proposals to the sharp tests of world-wide appraisal, thus reveal-
ing the strength, or weakness, of a cause that might otherwise
have remained hidden. It can activate the sound instincts of the
common man in favor of righteous causes. It can educate and
guide. But it has, also, weaknesses. There is the temptation to
play to the gallery at the expense of solid construction. And there
is the risk that positions once taken publicly become frozen,
making compromise more difficult.

Thus we find introduced in conference diplomacy an aspect of
propaganda and an element of rigidity which may be harmful to
sound negotiation. In these circumstances it is natural, and it
has been increasingly felt, that the balance to be struck within
the United Nations between conference diplomacy and quiet
diplomacy—whether directly between representatives of Member
governments or in contacts between the Secretary-General and
Member governments—has to be carefully measured and maintained. This balance should obviously be established in such a
way as to render the Organization as valuable an instrument as
possible for the achievement of progress toward peace. [28]

(Not the parties alone, but practically all the states in the world, are represented at the negotiating table in the United Nations. The parties thus have to meet both the arguments coming from the other side, and the judgments and reactions expressed by states which, even if not directly engaged, are interested. It is dangerous, and in my view highly presumptuous, to describe this situation as one in which the parties are confronted with "world opinion" and its "moral judgment" at the negotiating table in the United Nations. But it is true that within the Organization they are being forced to confront their stand with that taken by states for whom the principles of the Charter may weigh more heavily than direct or indirect partisan interests. [10]

❨ I think that the ten years that have passed have fully confirmed the belief of those who drafted the Charter in 1945 that in the post-war world a major role in diplomacy would have to be played by such *multilateral* negotiation which brings to bear the influence of other interested parties as well as those immediately engaged in a dispute, with the impact of their own experience, and with their perhaps less emotional and more detached viewpoints. [8]

❨ The United Nations system places at the disposal of the Member nations a wider diversity of influences and institutions favourable to peaceful settlement than has existed in the past. Its open debates give public opinion the opportunity to test the merits of the respective national positions on the issues before the Organization. In spite of what superficially and in a short perspective may often seem to be indications to the contrary, the debates generally tend in the long run to reduce the differences between these positions. [66]

❨ It is my hope that solid progress can be made in the coming years in developing new forms of contact, new methods of deliberation, and new techniques of reconciliation. With only slight adjustments, discussions on major issues of a kind that have occurred outside the United Nations could often be fitted into its framework, thus at the same time adding to the strength of the World Organization and drawing strength from it. There is, for example, the provision of the Charter, so far unused, for special periodic meetings of the Security Council. Might not this provision be invoked and procedures developed in the Council which would give increased continuity and intensified contact in the treatment of certain questions of world concern? [78]

⟪ After all, it is not too long ago that a famous phrase was coined, that "war is the ultimate resort of diplomacy." According to the United Nations philosophy, the United Nations ideology, war is in no sense the ultimate resort. War is bad. But then of course there must be an alternative. The United Nations alternative is clearly set out. [8]

⟪ Because it is more difficult to limit wars to a single area, all wars are of concern to all nations. Not only construction, but also destruction may today be global. [27]

⟪ The extent to which quiet diplomacy in preparation for the public diplomacy of the Security Council may be attempted will be largely dependent upon the general state of tension in the world. The less tension there is, the greater will be, I think, the chance for this kind of approach; the greater the tension, the stronger the tendency to bring out the differences in, so to say, their raw state at the first meeting of the Security Council on a controversial question. [8]

⟪ The United Nations is necessary because the classical forms of bilateral diplomacy are no longer sufficient in the world that has become ours. The Organization is necessary, moreover, because regional organizations alone cannot satisfactorily make up for these shortcomings of bilateral diplomacy. The Organization is necessary, finally, as a phase in the evolution toward those more definitive forms of international cooperation of universal scope which I, for one, am convinced must come, but which cannot be brought into being without many experiments and long pre-liminaries.

It is dangerous to overestimate the importance of personal contacts, but on the other hand it is unrealistic to underestimate the importance of the fact that qualified representatives of opposing camps live together, sharing their problems, and at the same time are in continuous touch with representatives of "uncommitted" governments. In these respects, as far as I am able to judge, things have developed further in New York than in any international centre in the past. [6]

❮ The permanent representation at Headquarters of all Member nations and the growing diplomatic contribution of the permanent delegations outside the public meetings—often in close contact also with the Secretariat—may well come to be regarded as the most important "common law" development which has taken place so far within the constitutional framework of the Charter. [17]

13

The Secretary-General

The office of the Secretary-General has been described as something like that of a secular pope; but while a pope has many precedents for his guidance, the Secretary-General has very few. Each man who has occupied the post has tended to mold it after his own image.

The Charter describes the Secretary-General as "the chief administrative officer in the Organization." He is responsible for the appointment of his staff members, and he alone is responsible for the principal organs—the three Councils and the General Assembly—for the efficient work of the Secretariat. The thousands of officials employed by the Organization must submit themselves to the rules of discipline laid down by him.

Up to this point, his functions are entirely administrative.

But the Charter entitles the General Assembly and the Security Council to entrust the Secretary-General with other functions involving the execution of political decisions. Moreover Article 99 of the Charter also says that "he may bring to the attention of the Security Council any matter which in his opinion may threaten the maintenance of international peace and security." In other words, he is to keep his eye out for trouble, and when he sees it brewing, he should make sure that action is taken.

The fact that the Secretary-General has political as well as administrative functions is reflected in the manner of his election.

He is selected by the Security Council where, since the veto may be applied to decisions, the great powers must unanimously agree upon him; this unanimity is needed because he deals with political and security matters. His name then goes before the General Assembly where he is elected, a demonstration that he owes allegiance not only to the Organization as a whole, but to each individual member.

On April 9, 1953, when Hammarskjöld arrived in New York, his predecessor, Trygve Lie, received him with these words: "Dag Hammarskjöld, you are going to take over the most impossible job in the world." Hammarskjöld immediately gave evidence that he looked upon his post as creative and dynamic. In a statement to the press he said, "In my new official capacity, the private man should disappear and the international public servant take his place. The public servant is there in order to assist, so to say from the inside, those who take decisions which frame history. . . . He is active as an instrument, a catalyst, perhaps an inspirer."

He was aware from the beginning of the uniqueness of his position, that of a diplomatic official with access to all governments and thus able to act in a way that no government and no national diplomat can do. He insisted that it was possible for the Secretary-General—who is after all a member of a nation state—to act, without subservience to a particular national or ideological attitude, as an honest broker between nations in controversy.

In the course of time, as he continued to define and redefine his amorphous post, the post became the image of Hammarskjöld. Whenever possible he put his abstract definitions into practice, and in so doing he developed new methods of leading the Organization step by step, hoping that, after they had been proved successful, his procedures might become part of the common law for organized international cooperation. A self-effacing man who preferred to work without publicity, he insisted that the Secretary-General must be self-effacing: "In nine cases out of ten, a Secretary-General would destroy his chances of exercising an independent influence on developments by publicly appealing to opinion over the heads of government." Thus he rarely communicated with the public and never became a popular figure; he thought of his office above all as that of a public servant.

When in 1957 he was reelected to a second term, he told the General Assembly: "Nobody, I think, can accept the position of Secretary-General of the United Nations, knowing what it means, except from a sense of duty. Nobody, however, can serve in that capacity without a sense of gratitude for a task as deeply rewarding as it is exacting, as perennially inspiring as, sometimes, it may be discouraging."

⟨ The Secretary-General of the United Nations is the Chief Administrative Officer of the Organization and, as such, the only elected member of the Secretariat. The founders of the United Nations may in this context have looked to the American Constitution. The chief of any government, or the Chief Executive in the United States, has the assistance of a group of close collaborators who represent the same basic approach, and to whom he therefore can delegate a considerable part of his responsibilities. On the basis of universality, especially in a divided world but generally speaking as long as nations have opposing interest, no similar arrangement is possible within the United Nations. [9]

⟨ The Secretary-General, as one of the main organs of the United Nations, shall have the opportunity of functioning as the spokesman of the Organization in its capacity as an independent opinion factor. [10]

⟨ I conceive the Secretariat and the Secretary-General in their relations with the governments as representatives of a secular "church" of ideals and principles of international affairs of which the United Nations is the expression. [23]

⟨ If negotiations are necessary, or if arrangements with a certain intended political impact are to be made, but member nations are not in a position to lay down exact terms of reference, a natural response of the Organization is to use the services of the Secretary-General for what they may be worth. [9]

❨ The diplomatic activity of the Secretary-General and his assistants is exercised in forms and for purposes which in many ways resemble those typical of the activity of an ambassador on behalf of his government, whether he is exercising "good offices" or operates as a negotiating party in relation to some other country.

When diplomatic efforts by the Secretary-General are increasingly demanded by Member governments, this must be taken as evidence that they have found it useful, in their relations with other states, to have available an outside party representing what might be called the common denominator. Often the Secretary-General has had to go into action where formerly a third government would have functioned, but where in this day and age, with present complex relations between governments, it has appeared simpler and more effective to turn to the Secretariat of the United Nations. [6]

❨ A positive influence, politically, for the Secretary-General can be imagined in practice only on two conditions. First, he must have the full confidence of the Member states, at least as to his independence and his freedom from personal motives. Second, he must accept the limitation of acting mainly on inner lines without publicity.

There are two possible lines of action for the Secretary-General in the political questions falling within the competence of the Organization, two lines which have both had their advocates in the debate about the office. The Secretary-General may interpret his constitutionally objective position in such a way as to refuse to indicate a stand in emerging conflicts in order thus to preserve the neutrality of the office. He may, however, also accord himself the right to take a stand in these conflicts to the extent that such stands can be firmly based on the Charter and its principles and thus express what may be called the independent judgment of the Organization. [10]

❲ He can take, backstage, all sorts of initiatives in order to convince the governments to avoid such and such a step that could complicate that situation. That way he may, as a kind of, let us say, senior diplomatic official, with the same access to all governments in the conflict, do something which no government itself could do and which none of the national diplomats could do.

His efficiency in these respects is in inverse proportion to the publicity he gives to what he does. The more he talks about it, the more distrustful, for obvious and natural reasons, governments are. The more quietly this kind of inner service on the different sides is pursued, the easier governments find it to use this service, and the further he can reach. [4]

❲ You may well guess—and you would be guessing correctly—that when I have the advantage of meeting these leading statesmen in various countries, usually the same pattern appears: the United Nations' problems in general—the UN and the world—on the one hand; and whatever local or regional problems are in the front of the minds of those statesmen. . . . Partly, those problems between countries are overlapping; partly, they are separate. But that is the pattern, and that much, of course, I can say without any indiscretion. [66]

❲ I have made it a rule never to refer directly to any conversation I have had with politicians behind closed doors—and I stick to it. [62]

❲ As the Secretary-General of the United Nations . . . with the special obligations of that office . . . I have to be like Caesar's wife: more than pure; that is to say, to guard even against unjustified suspicions. [66]

❲ The tasks . . . entrusted to the Secretary-General are mostly of such a character that, with the composition of an international Secretariat and of the group of his closest collaborators, with its naturally wide geographical distribution, he must carry out the work on a fairly personal basis. Obviously, there is no parallel to this in the field of national politics or diplomacy, and the case I have described, therefore, highlights one of those essential complications which characterize in the constitutional field the effort to work in the direction of organized international cooperation. [9]

❰ Because he has no pressure group behind him, no territory, and no parliament in the ordinary sense of the word, he can talk with much greater freedom, much greater frankness, and much greater simplicity in approaching governments than any government representative can do. [37]

❰ Whatever my personal ideology may be, I have certain obligations in relation to all the Member nations, and one primary obligation, of course, is to understand—without approval or disapproval—what the facts are and how they fit into the picture. [82]

❰ A Secretary-General cannot serve on any other assumption than that—within the necessary limits of human frailty and honest differences of opinion—all Member nations honor their pledge to observe all articles of the Charter. [33]

❰ I don't know if anyone is qualified for this job. You have to do as well as you can. [69]

❰ For someone whose job so obviously mirrors man's extraordinary possibilities and responsibilities, there is no excuse if he loses his sense of "having been called." [83]

It is for you to judge how I succeed,
it is for you to correct me if I fail. [69]

❨ It may be true that in a very deep, human sense there is no neutral individual, because, as I said at Oxford, everyone, if he is worth anything, has to have his ideas and ideals—things which are dear to him, and so on. But what I do claim is that even a man who is in that sense not neutral can very well undertake and carry through neutral actions, because that is an act of integrity. That is to say, I would say there is no neutral man, but there is, if you have integrity, neutral action by the right kind of man. [56]

❨ People have attached importance to the fact that I happen to come from one of the countries with traditional neutrality: Sweden. . . . I do not think that matters so much as the very good background training you get as active diplomat for a small country—a small country with a long foreign policy tradition—because that forces you to look at world problems in a fairly detached way. Your own country is not too much involved; you have a need to analyze as objectively as you can what are the interests at stake, what are the motives of the big powers, etc. I think that is a reasonable amount of good training. [69]

❨ "Neutrality" may develop, after all, into a kind of *jeu de mots*. I am not a neutral as regards the Charter; I am not neutral as regards facts. But that is not what we mean. What is meant by "neutrality" in this kind of debate is, of course, neutrality in relation to interests; and there I do claim that there is no insurmountable difficulty for anybody with the proper kinds of guiding principles in carrying through such neutrality one hundred per cent. [57]

❨ If the Secretary-General represents an independent but positive evaluation, free of partisan influences and determined by the purposes of the Charter, this means not only that he reinforces the weight that independent opinion may come to carry in the negotiations. Step by step, he thereby also builds up a practice which may open the door to a more generally recognized independent influence for the Organization as such in the political evolution. [10]

⟨[The Secretary-General . . . is duty bound to treat all Member nations alike, to maintain that kind of integrity and impartiality which makes it possible for him to make decisions without taking sides. [63]

⟨[Your position never gives you the right to command. It only imposes on you the duty of so living your life that others can receive your orders without being humiliated. [83]

⟨[In articles recently published it has been said that I am interested in mountaineering. . . . That much I know of this sport that the qualities it requires are just those which I feel we need today: perseverance and patience, a firm grip on realities, careful but imaginative planning, a clear awareness of the dangers but also of the fact that fate is what we make it and that the safest climber is he who never questions his ability to overcome all difficulties. [20]

⟨[In the multi-dimensional world of diplomacy, the Euclidean definition of the straight line as the shortest way between two points may not always hold true. For the Secretary-General, however, it is the only possible one. [15]

⟨["What is the competence of the SG?" Well, I could write a long paper on that in order to explain that it is much more than it looks on paper, and much less than people believe. [4]

⟨[The Secretary-General . . . is not out to "sell" anything. His is not a propaganda operation. But he has to try and reach the minds and hearts of people so as to get the United Nations' efforts firmly based in public reaction.

I cannot find any part of my present task more challenging than the one which consists in trying to develop all the potentialities of that unique diplomatic instrument which the Charter has created in the institution called the Secretary-General of the United Nations. [22]

(We have back of us the responsibility created by, in fact, centuries of development. We have in front of us millennia. And in between those centuries and those millennia there are a few years which we might measure in days and weeks and years and five-year terms of office of the Secretary-General, if I look at it from my angle, and those days are really nothing in comparison to what is back of us, and what is in front of us. But they get their sense from what is back of us, and they get their sense in what they mean for the future; that is to say, what we can hand over after our time of work is not just what we have managed to add to the heritage, it is the whole heritage with the little we have managed to add. [40]

(The motto of one of the old ruling houses in Europe was: "I serve." This must be the guiding principle, and also the inspiration and the challenge, for all those who have to carry the responsibility of office for any community. Is it not natural that this motto should be felt with special faith, sincerity, and loyalty by those who assist in the greatest venture in international cooperation on which mankind has ever embarked? [28]

(He broke fresh ground—because, and only because, he had the courage to go ahead without asking whether others were following or even understood. He had no need for the divided responsibility in which others seek to be safe from ridicule, because he had been granted a faith which required no confirmation.* [83]

(At the induction in my present office I quoted these lines by a Swedish poet: "The greatest prayer of man is not for victory, but for peace." Let this be the end of my words today also. [28]

*In *Markings* Hammarskjöld often referred to himself in the third person.

This House

Like the Secretary-General, the members of the Secretariat occupy unique positions whose functions and responsibilities have never been completely formulated. The Charter enjoins that besides "high standards of efficiency, competence and integrity," due regard should be paid to the importance of recruiting staff on a wide geographical basis. This rule has been maintained by the Communist nations, who feel themselves to be under-represented in the Secretariat.

Today new difficulties are in the making. The advent of newly independent nations has brought huge geographical areas under the United Nations umbrella, but their yield of efficient and competent personnel for the Secretariate is thin.

Staff members "shall not seek or receive instruction from any government or from any other authority external to the Organization." Member States, on their part, "shall not seek to influence staff members in the discharge of their responsibilities."

Neither in the League nor in the United Nations have these rules been kept. Hammarskjöld had not been in office a month before he found governments concerning themselves with the attitude of their nationals, slowing down the execution of agreements and the carrying through of decisions. He devoted much thought to the precise definition of an international civil servant and tried to formulate a code and a set of ideals for guidance.

Is it, after all, impossible in a divided world for members of an international Secretariat, coming from different nations, loyal to divergent ideologies and warring interests, to reliably serve a World Organization? Can one serve two masters? Is it paradoxical to remain true to one's personal ideals and yet act in the interests af a community of nations?

Hammarskjöld thought it was not paradoxical. A born mediator, he saw no difficulty in listening to one's own voice and in listening in all honesty to the many voices of the world. International life, he thought, far from demanding that we desert ideals basic to our personality, "puts us under an obligation to let those ideals and interests reach maturity and fruition in a universal climate."

To create unity in diversity: That was the goal he placed before the international civil service. He insisted that the Secretariat was more than a service organization: why else was it labeled a "main organ" in the Charter? It was also an executive body, having within itself special divisions such as technical assistance, specialized agencies, and very important regional economic organizations, all of which have power of intiative and negotiating rights.

He sought to transfer to the staff members his own sense of inner dedication; the United Nations was a "secular church," he said, with special ideals and principles regarding international affairs; the Secretary-General and the Secretariat were a priesthood whose mission was to lead the Organization toward the goals of the Charter.

"The weight we carry," said Hammarskjöld to his staff the year he took office, "is not determined by physical force of the number of people who form this constituency. . . . It is based solely on trust in our impartiality, in our experience and knowledge, our maturity of judgment. These qualities are our weapons. In no way secret weapons, but as difficult to forge as guns and bombs."

❨ Let us work in the conviction that our work *has* a meaning beyond the narrow individual one and *has* meant something for man. [58]

⟮ The international civil servant who works for an organization with members of different ideologies and interests remains under the obligation that applies to all of us—to be faithful to truth as he understands it. In doing so he is loyal—both in relation to the Organization and to his country. In doing so, he must, of course, subordinate himself to rules of good order, as all of us should do.

The concept of loyalty is distorted when it is understood to mean blind acceptance. It is correctly interpreted when it is assumed to cover honest criticism. [26]

⟮ The International Secretariat will not be what it is meant to be until the day when it can be recruited on a wide geographical basis without the risk that then some will be under—or consider themselves to be under—two masters in respect of their official functions. [56]

⟮ Nobody should use his position in an international organization for attacks on his own country or its policies, however strongly he may feel that he is right. Nor should anybody, as a national, attack the international organization for which he is working, and thereby place himself outside the discipline and the procedure established for the maintenance of that organization. [26]

⟮ The presence of the Secretariat established as a principal organ of the United Nations for the purpose of upholding and serving the international interest . . . can provide help not to be found elsewhere, if . . . rightly applied and used. [78]

⟮ Members of the secretariats must accept the international discipline that requires them to abstain from any political activity outside the scope of their duties and from any other activity which might throw doubt on their status as trusted and dedicated servants of the United Nations as a whole. On the other hand, on this basis the international civil service should be left free from national pressures of any sort. Only if this is so will the secretariats be able to render the service necessary to world organization. The United Nations itself cannot be fully effective in its appointed functions except under these conditions. [76]

❪ The international civil servant must keep himself under the strictest observation. He is not requested to be a neuter in the sense that he has to have no sympathies or antipathies, that there are to be no interests which are close to him in his personal capacity or that he is to have no ideas or ideals that matter for him. However, he is requested to be fully aware of those human reactions and meticulously check himself so that they are not permitted to influence his actions. This is nothing unique. Is not every judge professionally under the same obligation? [11]

❪ The Secretariat constantly has to analyse positions and problems; when asked to do so, it has to give the results of its analysis in terms of advice; and it has itself to use the opportunities which constantly arise to smooth out those unnecessary differences and misunderstandings which are bound to develop in a big world system.

The Secretariat is not a kind of super-diplomacy or super-Foreign Office. It is not even a coordinated organ of that kind. It is, in a very qualified sense, a service organization here too: it supplements, but it never competes with, the activities of Governments. It follows that the Secretariat, or the Secretary-General, never tries and never should try to tell any country, any Government, what it should do. Personally, I am firmly against any kind of attempt at policy-making through statements from the Secretary-General. And, finally, the Secretariat should not, unsolicited, mix into inter-State affairs in the sense of volunteering as a mediating body or something of that kind. If it is called upon, that is another matter.

Its function is to find and to keep alive and to broaden whatever may be the common denominator in the foreign policies of the nations. [8]

¶ The Charter requires of the Secretariat that it act without taking or seeking advice from Member governments. It follows that the assistance the Secretariat can give must be inspired only by the principles and aims of the Organization, independent of the special interests of any individual Members.

Because the Secretariat is a living thing—and its individual Members, with their own convictions and hopes, their own idealism, are independent of orders from any government—it is something more than a ticking mechanism. It has creative capacity. It can introduce new ideas. It can in proper forms take initiatives. It can put before the Member governments new findings which will influence their actions. Thus, the Secretariat in its independence represents an organ not only necessary for the life and proper functioning of the body, but of importance also for its growth. [28]

¶ It can fairly be said that the United Nations has increasingly succeeded in affirming the original idea of a dedicated professional service responsible only to the Organization in the performance of its duties and protected insofar as possible from the inevitable pressures of national governments. And this has been done in spite of strong pressures which are easily explained in terms of historic tradition and national interests. [56]

¶ I also felt that the first duty of the Secretary-General must be to give to the staff and to staff problems their proper priority in the efforts. How can you possibly go into the field of political activity, try your efforts in the diplomatic sphere, if you have a feeling that the very basis on which these efforts have to be developed is a weak one—not in the professional sense, but in the sense of human satisfaction in the job, human feeling of belonging to the joint effort? [41]

¶ I can tell you that during the three years I have been Secretary-General, not one single person has been fired for either political reasons or at the demand of any Member nation. [60]

¶ A truly international civil service, free from all national pressures and influences, should be recognized, not only in words, but in deeds. [76]

¶ Never, "for the sake of peace and quiet," deny your own experience or convictions. [83]

¶ Those who serve the Organization can take a pride in what it has done already in many, many cases. I know what I am talking about if I say, for example, that short of the heavy work in which each of you has had his or her part, the Congo would by now have been torn to pieces in a fight which in all likelihood would not have been limited to that territory, but spread far around, involving directly and indirectly many or all of the countries from which you come. I also know what the activities of the Organization in the economic and social fields have meant for the betterment of life of millions, and for the creation of a basis for a happier future.

Although the dangers may be great and although our role may be modest, we can feel that the work of the Organization is *the* means through which we all, jointly, can work so as to reduce the dangers. It would be too dramatic to talk about our task as one of waging a war for peace, but it is quite realistic to look at it as an essential and—within its limits—effective work for building dams against the floods of disintegration and violence. [58]

❡ We are not what we should be, we have not reached the full strength of our possible contribution, until we have managed to develop within ourselves, and in our relations with others, the sense of belonging. We are no Vatican, we are no republic, we are not outside the world—we are very much in the world. But, even within the world, there can be this kind of sense of belonging, this deeper sense of unity.

Whatever happens, stick to your guns, so that you can feel satisfaction with what you have done, whatever the outcome.

Our friends here were singing a Swedish song, the melody of which I think is very beautiful. The words are perhaps a little bit on the sad side. If I may translate the first line of the song, it runs like this: "Will the flowers of joy ever grow?" Those words, in fact, were taken up later by a Swedish poet, who developed the theme in a way which I would like to mention today as a kind of background for what I would like to say in conclusion. The poem culminates in the words: "Will the day ever come when joy is great and sorrow is small?"*

Looking at it in terms of humanity, looking at it in terms of the development of human society, it can be said, of course, that what we are trying to do here is to make our small contribution, during our short time, to a development which will finally lead us to the day "when joy is great and sorrow is small."

However, you can also look at those words in a much more personal and intimate sense. I think it is possible to interpret them superficially but it is also possible to interpret them in a sense which goes to the very heart of our way of settling our relation to life. And then I would say that, on the day we feel that we are living with a duty, well fulfilled and worth our while, on that day joy is great and we can look on sorrow as being small. [41]

*Gunnar Ekelof (b. 1907), member of the Swedish Academy, in the poem "Prästkrage säg." The song is an old Swedish folk song and was a favorite of Dag Hammarskjöld's.

15

The Press

Hammarskjöld never sought personal publicity. He regarded his profession of diplomacy as "basically something rather undramatic." The profession of journalism, on the other hand, requires that world news be presented in the press in a manner that will capture public attention. Friction between the Secretary-General and the press was bound to arise, and Hammarskjöld's position was often something like that of a shy and mild young man apologizing to hungry lions for not being able to deliver to them their daily Christian.

Though he admitted the right of newspaper men to claim full understanding of world affairs, he was wont to accuse them of "back-seat driving," and he kept reminding them that "in diplomacy and politics, the one in the back seat sees less of the road than the one at the wheel." The correspondents on the other hand complained that his "quiet diplomacy" and scarce press conferences kept United Nations affairs out of the mainstream of international news.

Nevertheless, as time passed, and the Secretary-General met year after year with the same reporters, an agreeable feeling of "belonging" grew up among them. When one reporter referred to Hammarskjöld's annual introduction to the Report to the General Assembly as "a State of the United Nations" message, he was pleased enough to give forth a spate of his shyly rambling

*phrases. He did not in the least object, he said, to turning his
press conference into a sort of Parliament "in which I am so to
say responsible in this particular way; I do not mind in any
sense."*

*He was, after all, a born front-seat driver, and he could not
be engaged with any group of people without wanting to lead,
and what's more, inspire them. He told the correspondents, "I
wish to enlist you as part of the Secretariat, working for the same
aims and ideals." And he added with unaccustomed warmth, "I
have been struck how deeply you feel yourselves engaged in that
venture in your activities as individuals. To use the word
'heartening' would be sentimental."*

❨ To translate diplomacy into that kind of language, into the
language of the daily press and the headlines of the daily press,
is not only a very difficult job, it is also a highly responsible job
because, as we know, finally, public opinion is one of the decisive
factors in the modern world—perhaps the most decisive factor in
the creation of policies, international policies in particular. [44]

❨ I have my professional duty to the seventy-six governments
which expect restraint from me in what I say publicly. . . . This
restraint is a little bit of a burden on me when I try to be helpful
to you, and you may find that even if I do not take recourse to
the famous phrase "no comment," some of my replies will be, let
us call it, somewhat evasive. [4]

❨ I am not very helpful in giving you stuff, either in the form of
news, statements or considered opinions, and what not. I try to
be helpful in other ways by explaining as well as I can on this
or that point how I really do look at this or that problem. [65]

❨ I would be overjoyed if I could give you, daily, good news
for the headlines. I would not be overjoyed to be able to give you,

daily, bad news. I may perhaps have a certain inclination, in view of the fact that bad news is likely to have greater interest than good news, to underplay the bad news at the expense of the good. [46]

⟨ It is really not for a slant in an optimistic direction, but for a very careful balance between good and bad news.

But I feel that . . . it is our duty . . . to approach the facts of the situation in this spirit, to avoid squeezing the possible drop of venom out of bad news. On the other hand, when something is said which is constructive, which is positive, which does indicate responsibility and perspective, one should give that, although it is good news and not bad news, just as much of a display as the bad news.

I think that by these very simple means, which are under our control, we can help those who work for peace, on this side or that side in the area, while on the other hand, by taking another line we do help the destructive forces, and that is so very much against what we want to do.

. . . Depart from what you think is realism, or what you think is truth, but avoid a dramatization in the direction of the devils and give God something.

The need for devoting so much time and energy to the political crises and problems that so often separate nations and regions should not be so time consuming as to cause us to neglect those large areas of life in which common ground of appreciation and understanding can be found.* [65]

*From Hammarskjöld's letter to correspondent David Horowitz, July 26, 1957.

❨ In the transition from thinking to speaking, something may be lost. In the transition from public speaking to the headlines of the papers of the world, very much is lost. It is unavoidable, and there is certainly no criticism in it of the way in which the world press serves the United Nations. I admire it. We get a coverage which is very encouraging—although not always flattering, but that is an entirely different matter. [8]

❨ QUESTION: Mr. Secretary-General, do you feel that the United Nations would have greater influence and impact on the world if there were stronger emphasis in the UN organs on moral condemnation of wrong-doers?

THE SECRETARY-GENERAL: I am perhaps not a moralist.

QUESTION: Am I correct in interpreting one of your recent speeches to mean that the United Nations constitutes the one hope and road to future world government?

THE SECRETARY-GENERAL: I have never used the words "the one hope for the world"—[48]

❨ I have taken in many respects a somewhat critical attitude to the trend of public debate on certain very burning issues. I have done so because I felt that really the trend of that discussion in its somewhat heated forms worked against not only our purposes but against what probably are the purposes which you want to serve yourself. [65]

16

The West and the Rest

In May 1959, in a speech before the Academic Association of the University of Lund in Sweden, Hammarskjöld ruminated about the changed relationship between Western Europeans and the rest of the world.

"I believe that no anthropologist nowadays," he said, "would say that the various branches of the family of man represent fundamentally different potentialities for . . . intellectual and material activity. . . . For my part, I have not been able to discover such differences."

Nineteenth-century Europe lived in unthinking self-centeredness. Goethe's concept of universality existed side by side with a firm conviction of the supremacy of the European man of culture, "a supremacy which erected invisible walls around his spiritual life in relation to other parts of the world."

Contact with Asian and African peoples which came about through the expanding empires did not break down the closed character of European culture. Since Asians and Africans were approached from a standpoint of "superiority," nothing they had to offer could be assimilated. Integration in such a setting was almost impossible. "To make it a reality required an intellectual humility and an openminded set of values" which came about only when "European man was shaken in his self-confidence and saw the walls around his closed world crumble before the pres-

sure of new forces which Europe itself in large part had called into being."
The First World War brought America into the picture. The Second World War opened the door to Asia and Africa. The European circle of culture now broke down, spiritually, politically, and geographically. Out of the chaos, a new synthesis on a universal basis had to be created, and this is the process we are witnessing today.
"One may reach back for the imagined calm of a closed world. One may find one's spiritual home in the very disintegration of its drama. Or, one may reach ahead toward the glimpse of the synthesis, inspired by the dream of a new culture."
It is evident that Hammarskjöld was inspired by that dream. No man more than he welcomed the newly independent countries as equal members into the family of nations. "No nation or group of nations can base its future on a claim of supremacy. It is in its own interest that the other groups should have equal opportunities."
For all that, he was aware of the weaknesses of the new nations. Leadership, he said, must be substituted for power— leadersship which assists without issuing commands. "The soundest way to perpetuate the cultural heritage of the West is to meet other peoples and other cultures in humble respect for the unique gifts they in turn have to offer humanity."

❨ The road has been opened to everyone in the most remote places of the globe to compare his position with that of more fortunate peoples. Thus, ideas and ideologies peculiar to the West have in our time, in their practical application, become factors in global development and of global significance. [43]

❨ The peoples of Asia today, of Africa tomorrow, are moving toward a new relationship with what history calls the West. The World Organization is the place where this emerging new relationship in world affairs can most creatively be forged. [78]

◖ I hope you do feel that this continent [Asia], and all its countries, really have a home in the United Nations, like all the other countries. There is no, so to say, inner temple somewhere the other side of the Pacific to which some have easier access than others. The temple is really all around the world and everyone is there in his own right. . . . That is the reason I am happy not only to come to Burma, but to Asia in general. It may bring home a little more clearly that this is the way we look at it. [75]

◖ You see when I come in this way, the main thing is, of course, not sightseeing, I am not a tourist and I have no right to be a tourist, the main thing is to meet people, broaden the contact beyond the scope which it has in New York. [4]

New Nations

The Charter states that the basic democratic principles are applicable to nations "large and small" and to individuals without distinction as to race, sex, language, and religion. The World Organization has assumed special responsibility to countries under colonial rule or in other ways under foreign domination.

"Nobody should minimize the admirable achievements frequently attained by colonizers," said Hammarskjöld, "but nobody should forget that colonization reflected a basic approach . . . which often mirrored false claims." And he pointed out that in many cases colonialism came to be represented by persons "whose only superiority over those they had to deal with lay in the power they had back of them." He quoted an Asian delegate who could see no reason whatsoever for his own country to remain a colony, since after many decades of Western rule, little progress was discernible.

During Hammarskjöld's tenure, many former colonies became independent nations, and he wholeheartedly supported their right to self-determination.

❰ Economic interdependence has been increasing rapidly. In part, this has been the inevitable outcome of advances in science and technology, in transport and communications, which tend not only to shrink physical distances but also to diffuse cultural patterns throughout the world community. The tendency has been reinforced by the powerful drive for national independence, beginning immediately after the war in Asia, and now reaching a rapid climax in Africa. Though in another context such a movement might have generated powerful centrifugal forces splitting peoples apart, in the context of responsible national and international statesmanship toward which the United Nations has undoubtedly made its contribution, the emergence of new nations has, in fact, been accompanied by a growing sense of sharing a common membership in a world community. [51]

⟮ It is natural for old and well-established countries to see in the United Nations a limitation on their sovereignty. It is just as natural that a young country, a country emerging on the world stage, should find in the United Nations an addition to its sovereignty, an added means of speaking to the world. [82]

⟮ It is a positive factor in the world of today that new countries do not stand isolated, but can immediately enjoy the advantages and facilities of an international community which has been able to develop certain principles and rules of behavior as well as a diversified institutional system, and which offers a framework where new friendships can be easily and rapidly gained while historic links can continue to develop on a basis of equality, purged of their former exclusiveness. [16]

⟮ It is my conviction that the addition of a great number of new Member States will widen the perspectives, enrich the debate and bring the United Nations closer to present-day realities. I also believe that this development will exercise a sound influence in the direction of a democratization of proceedings by lessening the influence of firm groupings with firm engagements. [18]

⟮ There is something very shocking in the idea that new States

must take so-called irresponsible stands. I myself do not believe
it for a moment. On the contrary, I believe that new States are
likely to approach problems with very great seriousness and with
a very great sense of responsibility. But, as I said before, it is
quite natural that they, like all of us, will have to find their way
through a political system and a framework of procedures which
so far have been unknown to them. [50]

❪ I do not believe that the small nations have less of an understanding of central political problems of concern to the whole
world than those who are more closely related to them and who
traditionally wield greater power in the international councils.
For that reason, I cannot—and this is not only the official stand
taken by the Secretary-General, it is a matter of personal conviction—share the view of those who regard the possible influence
of smaller Powers as a danger—I would add, in any context. [7]

❪ In the pride of self-realization natural to these new states we
should welcome the constructive element—a self-assertion like
that of a young man coming of age, conscious of his powers,
eager to find his own way, to make his voice heard, and to render
his contribution to progress. [27]

❪ The dominant mood of the peoples of these continents is often
described as nationalism. This is a fair enough description. But
the real basis of this great change goes deeper, I think. There is
back of it also a desire to countries of Asia and Africa to see
applied what the Charter calls "the equal rights of men and
women and of nations large and small."

It is also sometimes said that the representation in the United
Nations of the nations of Asia and Africa, many of them newly
independent, is out of proportion to their power and tends to
exacerbate the many problems of transition in the relationship
of these continents to the West, especially to Europe. . . . In the

United Nations we see reflected the political rebirth of Asia and the awakening of Africa. But the United Nations, of course, is in no sense a cause of these great changes. [13]

¶ History places a burden on our shoulders. The creative urges of the emergent nations are tinged with strong emotions from the past. It is for all of us, denying neither the good nor the ills of that past, to look ahead and not to permit old conflicts to envenom the spirit of the creative work before us. [27]

¶ The fifteen years which have passed since the founding of the United Nations have witnessed a different development. In the first place, we have seen a split among the permanent members which, in fact, has created the major war risk of today and considerably hampered the development of the Organization. But, further, we have experienced a growth into independence of a majority of States of two continents, with other interests, other traditions, and other concepts of international politics than those of the countries of Europe and the Americas. Who can deny that today the countries of Asia or the countries of Africa, acting in a common spirit, represent powerful elements in the international community, in their ways as important as any of the Big Powers, although lacking in their military and economic potential?

Neither size, nor wealth, nor age is historically to be regarded as a guarantee for the quality of the international policy pursued by any nation.

It is my conviction that the addition of a great number of new Member States will widen the perspectives, enrich the debate, and bring the United Nations closer to present-day realities. [18]

¶ There is a maturity of mind required of those who give up rights. There is a maturity of mind required of those who acquire new rights. Let us hope that, to an increasing extent, the necessary spiritual qualities will be shown on all sides. [11]

18

Africa

The United Nations, as it was conceived in San Francisco, has been hampered and weakened by great power conflicts and the Cold War. With the emergence of Africa, Hammarskjöld saw a powerful new force arriving upon the international arena. He traveled widely in the Dark Continent and reported the lessons he learned there. Personal contact and personal experience filled him with some "feeling of concern" as well as with an "enormous sense of encouragement." The two problems to be solved are to "create an international world, a world of universality and unity, and on the other hand to save not only the 'personality of Africa' but the personality of each country and each group.

"What is needed is unity in diversity and diversity respected within the framework of an even greater respect for unity."

He met remarkable leaders, "but they were few"; and he said, "Quality will have to make up for numbers and quantity."

In his cross-continental tours he observed that political borders often cut across natural economic regions in a manner that made their development impossible. Such countries, he thought, would have to devise means of acting in concert, without, however, any form of political integration or federation being imposed upon them.

He called for all Member nations to cooperate in shaping the future of the continent: personnel were needed, and so were

*money and civic education to bring people not only to national
awareness, but to a point "where they can form, as free individuals,
their judgment on political issues."*

*Finally, they needed moral support. "In fact, I guess that is the
most significant, because people and money and education do not
mean a thing unless they are given and provided in the right
spirit."*

*By moral support, he meant a sympathetic understanding of the
problems of peoples and their leaders, "neither a feeling of false
superiority, nor a feeling of sterile pessimism, nor a feeling of
facile optimism." What is needed, he told his press conference in
February 1960, is "understanding joined with something which
really helps."*

*"Why shouldn't it be provided by all Member States of the
United Nations and by the Organization itself?"*

⟨ The great changes that are under way in Africa present a
challenge to the rest of the world—a challenge to give aid in guiding the course of events in orderly and constructive channels. It
is apparent that in the next ten years the peace and stability of
the world will be strongly affected by the evolution in Africa,
by the national awakening of its people, by the course of race
relations, and by the manner in which the economic and social
advancement of the African peoples is assisted by the rest of the
world. [78]

⟨ The African States have realized that to grow into independence
means to grow into interdependence. But to grow into interdependence means also to assume international responsibility, and
such international responsibility must be based on national responsibility. [18]

⟨ I do, for my part, believe that the usefulness of the United
Nations will be increased by the addition of African States to
the General Assembly. I do believe very much in the ability of

those various states to make valuable contributions as soon as they have found their way in the maze of the United Nations. And I have already said at a previous press conference that their admission will move the General Assembly more in the direction of a true democratic parliament than we have had so far. I believe that in that way they will add life to the debates and to the consideration of questions. [46]

(The Organization must further and support policies aiming at independence, not only in the constitutional sense but in every sense of the word, protecting the possibilities of the African peoples to choose their own way without undue influences being exercised and without attempts to abuse the situation. This must be true in all fields—the political, the economic, as well as the ideological—if independence is to have a real meaning.

The attitude is one of willingness to cooperate with the rest of the world and one of eagerness to integrate into the rest of the world, combined, however, with a firm rejection of any attempts by others to turn the efforts of the African states to achieve this cooperation and integration into subjection, be it political, economic, or ideological.

Finally, in Africa the first beginnings can now be seen of those conflicts between ideologies and interests which split the world. Africa is still, in comparison with other areas, a virgin territory which many have found reason to believe can or should be won for their aims and interests.

The United Nations . . . appealed to "African solidarity within the framework of the United Nations." As the developments have shown, this is not a mere phrase; it applies to something which has become a reality. It is my firm conviction that the African states cannot render themselves and their peoples a greater service than to foster this solidarity. Likewise, I am convinced that the United Nations cannot render its new African Member States and the whole community of nations in Africa a greater service than to assist them, within the framework of their own efforts, to mold their new national and regional life, now that they enter the community of nations, in ways that will give Africa its rightful place on the international scene.

It is for the African states themselves to define the elements which establish the basis for African solidarity. It is also for them to find and define the aims which this regional community should pursue. [18]

⟨ It is a somewhat superficial and sometimes misused expression to talk about an African renaissance, but I think that the word can be taken in a much deeper sense and here, in a setting where thoughts naturally go to Italy or the Renaissance, I think it is right to recall things which this time and that time have in common.

It is not only the vitality, it is not only width of perspective, it is also the emerging strong sense of the dignity of man, of the dignity of the individual and of his rights. There are many features in the present situation in Africa and among its leaders, and among its young people, which unavoidably lead our thoughts to great men of that time in Italy and in Europe. That time was also the time of a new resurgence of learning; and, going around Africa and meeting these people, I would say that one of the things which have struck me most is the keen sense of responsibility for a widened and intensified education as a basis for the present phase in the development of Africa.

It is an enormous task which is facing our African friends. . . . They will face an interesting and two-fold problem which, alas, I am not sure that the European Renaissance solved in the right spirit. The ideas were there, but the solutions were not always the happiest. The two problems they will have to solve is to create an international world, a world of universality and unity, and on the other hand to save not only what I would like to call the personality of Africa, but the personality of each country, each group, in this wonderfully rich continent.

I think it is possible; I think it is possible because also, my African friends, you can learn from mistakes in other parts of the world, in other phases of history. I think that you will see that what is needed is unity with diversity, diversity respected within the framework of an even deeper respect for unity. You *can* create, and I know you will create, the African personality as part of the picture of mankind today. But I know that, in doing so, you will preserve all the richness you have inherited; each group, each people within this continent. [45]

❮ I had the privilege of visiting some few of the great universities in Africa, and I must say that I admire their work. It is, as I said about the chief political leaders and administrators, a question of very high standards indeed, but again quality has to make up for the lack in quantity.

Education is also the method through which you get the doctors, the engineers, the administrators and, to some extent, of course, also the political leaders, although I do not believe that there, any more than other places, the universities will be the main breeding ground for political leaders; political leaders, after all, are mostly made in the field, in practical life. [46]

❮ Education is not only broad education at the bottom; it is not school teaching and book learning. It is civic education. It is the methods by which you bring people not only to national awareness but to the point where they form as free individuals their judgment on political issues. [64]

❮ We all know the present scope and pace of the emergence of African countries and territories into political independence. It is essential that African economic growth acquire sufficient momentum to match the pace of political change. The early period of independence may in this respect prove decisive. [14]

❮ Problems confronting the African states are, in a great measure, the same problems that confront most of the under-developed areas, whether they have been independent for some time or have not yet reached their complete sovereignty. They are the problems of disease and illiteracy; of economies dominated by the production for export of a small range of primary products; of countries with a still large subsistence sector more or less isolated from the local and world markets. [16]

❨ The new Economic Commission for Africa will strengthen the influence of the United Nations in an area where political tensions are likely to become higher in the years immediately ahead, and it can help to a considerable extent in reducing these tensions. [13]

❨ It is something very striking that from the far west coast and to the south east coast as a belt all across Africa south of the Sahara, there is one standing demand, one standing hope. It is less for money or for experts, because those countries know very well that we haven't got much money and we are not likely to get much money in this Organization. It is much more for what I have called here the moral support which is expressed even in the most modest action through the right people.

It is not decisive that tens or hundreds of times more money will come through other channels; although frankly I would, as I said before, prefer to see it go through United Nations channels, because it does make the money more effective, it does help the receiving country by more than the money. It helps it also in its effort to find its place on the world map. [64]

❨ I believe that this is an area of concern to the United Nations in which the Secretariat may prove helpful. As a first step in the Secretariat approach it is essential to bring together and into focus the many problems concerning Africa with which the United Nations is already dealing or will have to deal in the years ahead. For this purpose, I have established a Secretariat working party to advise me. [78]

19

One Nation, One Vote

There is a flaw inherent in any kind of universal suffrage: One may wonder if it is right that the vote of the Dean of the Columbia Law School has precisely the same weight as that of his cleaning-woman. At the United Nations, undeveloped countries such as the Upper Volta and Dahomey have the same vote value as the United States and the Soviet Union, and fears have been voiced that the efficiency of the Organization is thereby impaired.

"Weighted voting" has been suggested as a solution. This would mean that Member nations would not have equal voice in the making of decisions. The votes of each would be weighed according to population, resources, power, contribution to the United Nations budget, and various other factors.

Hammarskjöld did not share this anxiety. While admitting that equal voting has practical drawbacks, he believed that "the advantages outweigh the disadvantages." In weighted voting we would lose something very essential: "the true application of the democratic principle expressed in the Charter—the equal right of each Member state, large or small."

Nor did he see more than temporary difficulties in bloc-voting. While in most instances the Soviet bloc votes together, the large Afro-Asian group on the other hand does not. He looked forward to a time when cohesion within blocs would lessen, and with the easing of tensions individual Members would act more separately.

Moreover, in time of crisis he placed his confidence in the efficacy of private negotiation rather than in the mechanics of voting. The public speeches culminating in votes were interesting, he thought, mainly as a forum. In his introduction to the Annual Report for 1961 he wrote, "A voting victory or a voting defeat may have short-lived significance. . . . Responsible world opinion, as reflected in the voting and in the debates, is in many respects more important than any formally registered result."

⟨ The General Assembly is a body which reflects in its decisions on major questions the results of long and careful negotiations and consideration. During this process, common lines are elaborated and compromises reached which give to the decisions the character of a confirmation of a negotiated approach rather than of a solution achieved through the mechanics of voting. [18]

⟨ Resolutions often reflect only part of what has, in fact, emerged from the deliberations and what, therefore, is likely to remain as an active element in future developments. In these circumstances, it is natural for those who are not close to the United Nations sometimes to underestimate the results of the work of the General Assembly and other organs, and equally to overestimate the significance of a formal voting victory or a voting defeat. [17]

⟨ In an organization of sovereign States, voting victories are likely to be illusory unless they are steps in the direction of winning lasting consent to a peaceful and just settlement of the questions at issue. [38]

⟨ There have been discussions about this or that kind of weighted voting. It is one of those ideas which have come up in discussions about a revision of the Charter. I think that we would lose something very essential if we were to abandon the present system. We may be ripe for weighted voting when we are ripe for world government. Then, of course, the weight should be the weight in the democratic sense of the word, not for the national state as such but for what the national state represents of mankind. But as long as we base international cooperation on the representation of sovereign national states, I feel that the only true application of the democratic principle is to uphold the equal right of each Member nation.

We have seen and will see again and again that the open airing of conflicts means that those who have a just cause have an opportunity to appeal to world conscience. People all over the world are sensitive to arguments which bring injustice out into the open and show that might, in some cases, has been stronger than right. In order to make it possible for the General Assembly to serve in this way for an appeal to world conscience in the cases where such an appeal is justified by facts, we must have the democratic parliamentary procedure; that is to say, an equal right to the floor for everybody and an equal influence on the decisions of everybody in the technical sense of voting. [8]

⟨ There is no practical alternative in keeping with the basic tenets of the Charter to the present system of equal votes for all sovereign Member States. [18]

⟨ In interstate politics, we are still only at the beginning of an evolution toward a system where a minority is presumed to bow to a majority. The normal thing in international deliberations remains, of course, agreement. [6]

20

Veto

Each of the five permanent members of the Security Council—China, France, the United Kingdom, the Soviet Union, and the United States—has veto power. No decision can be taken by that body on a matter of substance unless these five permanent members vote for it unanimously. A negative vote by any one of them kills the resolution. The procedure was agreed upon in 1945 at Yalta by Roosevelt, Churchill, and Stalin, and though it was hotly debated by lesser powers at San Francisco where the United Nations was born that same year, and efforts have since been made to modify it, the great power veto is still with us, sometimes paralyzing action by the Council.

The Soviet Union, being the only socialist power among the permanent members and thus easily outvoted, has made by far the most frequent use of the veto; and some have called it abuse.

Hammarskjöld certainly did not love any paralyzing mechanism, but he did not think it was possible to abolish the veto power, and since it was there he made the best of it. In 1956 in New Delhi, speaking to the Indian Council of World Affairs, he pointed out that it actually offers a certain protection to small powers, guaranteeing that they cannot be dragged into military or police action—or any other action—by a majority decision of the Security Council, when there was no unanimity of opinion among the great powers.

He agreed with Krishna Menon who said, "The day we get rid of the veto, there will be no reason to get rid of it." It is obvious that the very day the great powers agree to relinquish the veto, they will have reached such a state of concord that the veto can no longer operate as a major obstacle to action. Nevertheless Hammarskjöld distinguished between use and abuse of the veto. There was such a thing as the "real veto" properly applied to problems which cannot be solved except by complete agreement among the great powers; and an "artificial veto" where one power attempts to make its consent essential in matters which should logically be solved on a majority basis.

❨ "When will the United Nations be what it was meant to be?"—where the Big Powers are agreed, two things will happen. The small countries will not need the protection of the veto; nor will the veto be used by the Big Powers; and for that reason it will be a dead-letter. But as long as we cannot count on unanimity in the approach to world problems between the Big Powers, I think we cannot get rid of the veto, and I think there is nothing to be said for it also from the point of view of the small countries in view of the very far-reaching rights of the Security Council. [4]

❨ Harsh words have been said about the use or abuse of the veto; sometimes there seems to me to be a tendency to underestimate the difficulties for the countries possessing the veto right to maintain their line of action in the Council in a way that is faithful to their opinions, without having recourse to the veto. However, the practical question is: Is there any reason to do away with the veto, is there any possibility even to do away with it? I think everybody is agreed that at present the veto could not be abolished, and I doubt whether it would be really desirable to abolish the veto. We must not forget that the veto, from the point of view of those countries which are not permanent members of the Security Council, is a guarantee that decisions taken by the Security Council are unanimous as among the permanent members. Some of the functions of the Security Council involve very heavy responsibilities for all Members of the United Nations, very heavy responsibilities in the military field, in the field of sanctions, police actions and so on. It should not be forgotten that for those countries whose hands would be tied by a decision of the Security Council, it does mean something that there is unanimity of the permanent Members behind the decision. [8]

21

Cold War

"You may feel that I am a blue-eyed fool believing in all sorts of things," said Dag Hammarskjöld to newspapermen, "but I do believe in possibilities. . . . I am an optimist."

Optimism was his stock in trade. In private he may have given way to despair and dark forebodings, but these concerned his own fate. For the world he did not envision inevitable doom.

The Cold War which divided the nations into competing power blocs was a thorn in his side. When conflicts arose within the orbit of these blocs, action by the Security Council and the General Assembly was quite often paralyzed. Hammarskjöld was therefore alert for opportunities to solve problems before they became entangled in bloc differences.

Power blocs too have an interest in keeping an area of conflict within controllable bounds and avoiding outright confrontation. In such cases a situation develops known as a "vacuum"—a place where angels fear to tread but blue-eyed fools do not. It was Hammarskjöld's design that the United Nations, uncommitted to any power bloc, should stand ready at all times to "fill the vacuum," preventing any action of the major parties from expanding to a clash.

Such preventive diplomacy was successfully accomplished in Suez and Gaza, Lebanon and Jordan, Laos, and the Congo.

⟨ The weakness of the United Nations is not anything which is explained by specific features in the Organization. It is just a reflection of the weakness of our present-day political situation. The United Nations, as you know, was framed on the idea that the five big powers should stand united in the common interest of peace. That is to say, when first the Cold War started and later the complication arose concerning the fifth member, China, one of the basic assumptions of the work of the United Nations broke down. [60]

⟨ With its constitution and structure, it is extremely difficult for the United Nations to exercise an influence on problems which are clearly and definitely within the orbit of present-day conflicts between power blocs. If a specific conflict is within that orbit, it can be assumed that the Security Council is rendered inactive, and it may be feared that even positions taken by the General Assembly would follow lines strongly influenced by considerations only indirectly related to the concrete difficulty under consideration. [18]

⟨ I consider it a very natural function for the Secretary-General to keep problems as much as possible outside the Cold War orbit and on the other hand, of course, to lift problems out of the Cold War orbit to all the extent he can. . . . It is one way, so to say, if not to thaw the Cold War, at least to limit its impact on international life. [48]

⟨ Experience indicates that the preventive diplomacy, to which the efforts of the United Nations must thus to a large extent be directed, is of special significance in cases where the original conflict may be said either to be the result of, or to imply risks for, the creation of a power vacuum between the main blocs. Preventive action in such cases must in the first place aim at filling the vacuum so that it will not provoke action from any of the major parties.

In all cases, whatever the immediate reason for the United Nations initiative, the Organization has moved so as to forestall developments which might draw the specific conflict, openly or actively, into the sphere of power bloc differences. It has done so by introducing itself into the picture, sometimes with very modest means, sometimes in strength, so as to eliminate a political, economic, and social, or military vacuum.

The ways in which a vacuum can be filled by the United Nations so as to forestall such initiatives differ from case to case, but they have this in common: temporarily, and pending the filling of a vacuum by normal means, the United Nations enters the picture on the basis of its noncommitment to any bloc, so as to provide to the extent possible a guarantee in relation to all parties against initiatives from others.

There is a field within which international conflicts may be faced and solved with such harmony between the power blocs as was anticipated as a condition for Security Council action in San Francisco. Agreement may be achieved because of a mutual interest among the Big Powers to avoid having a regional or local conflict drawn into the sphere of bloc politics. [18]

⟨ The present divisions of our world often appear unbridgeable and the obstacles to ultimate agreement insurmountable. But the landscape of international affairs is not immutable. It is constantly shifting and moving, subject to all the influences at work in our world, in which new opportunities develop and the hope for ultimate solutions can never be abandoned. [76]

⟨ Let us not overlook the ideological tensions, but, on the other hand, let us not exaggerate their significance. Especially, let us not get caught in the belief that divisions of our world between the righteous and the wrong-doers, between idealism and boundaries. The righteous are to be found everywhere—as are the wrong-doers. Those whose only ideal is material well-being meet us in every country—as those whose ideal is selfless service. [25]

22

Politics

The general public does not hold politics in high esteem; some of us, when speaking of politicians, have a hard time not tucking in the adjective "crooked" or "dumb." But Hammarskjöld said, "There is no intellectual activity which more ruthlessly tests the solidity of a man than politics."

He had a warning, though, about the danger of a "politicized world" and he chose to give it, of all places, at a state dinner of the United States Governors Conference in 1958. He said that in a world where politics is the concern of everyone, a danger exists that propaganda becomes more important than substance, and that the politician himself may lose the ability to communicate sincerely—especially with those who hold different views—and he may forget also how to listen to their arguments. To the extent that this can happen, "the politicized world becomes a dehumanized world." This explains in part the seeming paradox that "no single people wants anything but peace, and no single government would take the responsibility of starting a war, but . . . all the same the world situation, politically, represents a picture of interlocking stalemates."

As Secretary-General he noted that political leaders (and spiritual leaders too) tend to be more trusting and conciliatory in private than in public. They fear that in public their more reasonable stand might not be understood, or might be abused by the opposition party, or misrepresented as a sign of weakness. "And so," he added with some melancholy, "the game goes on—toward an unforeseeable conclusion. . . ."

❨ A "politicized" world is a world where individual reactions have to be disciplined and subordinated to group interests, and where, for that reason, conformism easily becomes an ideal. It is a world where tactics often are given priority over substance and in which, for this reason, we may lose sight of the real interests in our search for propaganda points to be scored. To use a comparison, it is also a world where the preacher may be tempted to give greater effort to winning the approval of the converted than to converting the sinners. [12]

❨ The end of all political effort must be the well-being of the individual in a life of safety and freedom. . . . The means to this end are in the first place the independence, peace, integrity, and prosperity of the country. In turn, this goal requires the maintenance and progress of economic life, the functioning of a good judiciary system, a soundly working administration, all under the responsibility of a government, stable thanks to its firm roots in the free will of the people, expressed and developed in democratic forms. [70]

❨ Politics and diplomacy are no play of will and skill where results are independent of the character of those engaging in the game. Results are determined not by superficial ability but by the consistency of the actors in their efforts and by the validity of their ideals. . . . Apparently easy successes with the public are possible for a juggler, but lasting results are achieved only by the patient builder. [26]

❨ Anyone who today tries to disengage himself from the political aspects of life cuts himself off from developments of the deepest direct significance for his own destiny. [12]

23

Living Standards

"Preventive diplomacy" as practiced by the World Organiza-
tion should not be limited, Hammarskjöld thought, to politics.
As an economist in a unique political position, he saw the firmest
foundation for peace in steadily expanding production, trade,
and consumption. Economic and social problems should rank
with political ones—in fact they should, if anything, have
priority. "While the Security Council exists primarily to elimi-
nate conflicts," he said in New Delhi in 1956, "the Economic and
Social Council exists primarily to eliminate causes of conflicts
by working to change those conditions in which emotional, eco-
nomic, and social background for conflict develops."

In his introduction to the Annual Report for 1959–1960, he
wrote, "In the end the United Nations is likely to be judged not
so much by the criterion of how successfully it has overcome this
or that crisis, as by the significance of its total contribution
toward building the kind of world community in which such
crises will no longer be inevitable."

(International equality and justice are prerequisites of the
domestic social development of all the peoples of the world and,

together, they are the decisive factors if we are to build a world of peace and freedom. No system of collective security can be built with sufficient strength unless the underlying pressures are reduced—and those pressures can be mastered only to the extent that we succeed in meeting the demands for international justice or internal social justice. [76]

⟨ It is for society to shoulder its responsibility in the fight against poverty, disease, inequality, and lack of freedom, by the means put at its disposal by science and technology. It is, likewise, the duty of society to shoulder the responsibility for the development of ways in which men can live together in this shrunken world, turning the dynamics of change into the stability of peace. [43]

⟨ The firmest foundation for a peaceful and stable world order is one of steadily expanding world production, trade, and consumption where inequalities of wealth and living standards among different parts of the world are diminishing while the general level is rising. [76]

⟨ I believe the time has come for the United Nations to deal more directly with—or at least to serve in a more systematic way as a forum for the consideration of—major international economic policies. [17]

⟨ The United Nations cannot consider itself disinterested in the successes and failures of domestic economic policies in the countries of Member States—the more so because social progress, which is one of the conditions for social stability and peace, will to a large extent depend on the ability of governments to develop a sound national economy. [77]

⟨ A generation ago, it might have been assumed that responsibility for policies of economic growth should be exclusively national. Today, such a premise is hardly tenable. This is already recognized in the United Nations Charter which reflects a major transformation of the concept of international cooperation and clearly establishes a measure of collective responsibility in such matters. Post-war experience has amply justified the Charter in this respect. It has been repeatedly shown that even a moderate slowdown in the rate of economic activity in one or two leading countries may affect prices and income, production and employment, and even prospects for development, in many parts of the world.

Through a rationally organized process of consultations, the Organization might, more than any other agency, play an important role in both the harmonization of national policies and the formulation of international objectives.

Consultations on long-term objectives and policies should not be mistaken for world economic planning. It is implicit in the Charter that each country shall give its own meaning to the objectives of full employment, economic growth, and price stability, in accordance with its own economic resources, its social and political institutions, and its cultural traditions. Consultations are only a means of arriving at a more effective and realistic formulation of these objectives and of the policies necessary for their attainment. [51]

⟦ The Organization will be able to make an important contribution toward widening the bounds of the area of coincidence of interest within the United Nations, thus helping to harmonize decisions of governments in the field of national policy and in the promotion of rapid and stable economic development for all. [18]

⟦ The United Nations cannot, and should not, interfere with, nor exert pressure on, domestic policies, but it can assist in the framing of such policies by providing careful analyses of the problems involved and guidance as to the international economic framework within which such policies have to be pursued. [77]

❨ The coincidence of interest in the economic field stems from the economic interdependence of the world community. The degree of interdependence has been increasing rapidly, partly as the inevitable outcome of an accelerating rate of advance in science and technology, partly owing to the emergence of the countries of the continents of Asia and of Africa to independence and full participation in the affairs of the world at large, but, to a significant degree, also as a result of economic forces making for a growing integration of the world community. [18]

❨ The world economic system which existed before the two world wars of the present century has been badly shaken. We are far from having established such conditions as would permit of a return of free trade, free movements of capital, and free movements of population. [77]

❨ It is necessary to remember that international economic equilibrium must be sufficiently dynamic and flexible to provide for the attainment of the three interrelated economic goals of the Charter: higher standards of living, full employment, and economic development. Any economic balance which fails to provide for satisfactory progress toward these goals would be a false balance and could not be maintained. [78]

❨ Just as it is clearly within the interests of the entire world community to prevent the widening of the area of conflict in cases of political crises, so it must be in the interests of all constantly to seek to widen rather than to restrict the area of coincidence of economic interest within the United Nations. Unless this is done, the entire world, and not just one or the other side, is bound to lose. [18]

❡ The problem of growth is not only a national one. It has inter-national implications which must always be kept in mind when decisions are made on the national economic policy to be pur-sued. An expanding world economy is of the highest importance to under-developed countries, since growth rates in industrial countries, through their impact on import demand for primary products, also go far to determine the potential rate of expansion in under-developed countries. This is why a policy in the indus-trial countries achieving stability at the cost of growth must be viewed with special concern by the under-developed countries.

First and foremost, appropriate domestic policies in the under-developed countries themselves are an essential prerequisite for healthy economic development. [17]

❡ The mere recognition of the community of interest in the economic development of under-developed countries itself rep-resents a major step forward. [18]

❡ The Organization can, as the only tool of its kind available to the governments of Members, make an essential contribution in developing a policy which in due time will raise the economically under-developed areas to a level where they will take their proper place in world trade and find a basis for a progressive social policy giving their populations a fair share in the growing wealth of the world. [77]

❡ Shortage of domestic capital continues to be a major obstacle to the economic development of the industrially less-advanced countries, and the need to increase the international flow of both private and public capital funds far above the present level is more apparent than ever.

The necessary increase in the flow of capital can come only

from the industrially advanced nations. We may feel that the hope of such an increase is related to an evolution in the world political climate releasing for constructive purposes some part of the resources now devoted to armaments. Nevertheless, the recent advances in the world economy to which I have referred should make possible a beginning even now. A substantial increase in the capital resources made available to the under-developed countries would represent only an insignificant fraction of the capital accumulated each year in the industrial countries. Such investments could bring, over a period of years, economic and political benefits that would more than justify a bold approach to the problem. [78]

⟨ From the point of view of the under-developed countries the provision of capital through United Nations agencies is in itself a guarantee of its nonpolitical character. From the point of view of the capital-exporting countries, the use of United Nations agencies as the vehicle for both private and public loans offers for the investor a safeguard that is backed by the moral weight of the whole community of nations. [76]

⟨ For the first time in history, the concept of a world economy has come to take on a significant meaning not only for the student of economics but also for the statesman and the layman. [18]

24

Population Explosion

"Population explosion" is the sort of catchy expression that Hammarskjöld did not generally use, but he was alert to the danger of rapidly growing population in a world where the fertility of man outraces the fertility of the land.

Today one third to one half of the world's inhabitants go to bed hungry. The situation is most acute in those under-developed areas where population is dense and resources meager, and where, since manpower rather than machines is needed to culti-vate the land, large families are an economic asset—and at the same time a liability.

Even developed areas face growing shortages as medical sci-ence continues to reduce the rate of infant mortality and to extend the span of life.

No nation can fight the danger of mass starvation alone. It is a global problem which must be fought globally. It is the concern of agencies, working within the framework of the Economic and Social Council, in agriculture, health, technical assistance, edu-cation, and trade. Dag Hammarskjöld the economist interested himself particularly in this work.

❰ World population is increasing at an unprecedented rate. In many countries it seems likely that the population will be doubled in a little more than twenty years. The movement from rural to urban centres continues and urban populations are thus being increased at a rate disproportionate to the absorptive capacity of the towns. A rate of economic growth which, in other circumstances, would be considered satisfactory is barely sufficient to maintain individual levels of living in under-developed countries. [17]

❰ Various United Nations surveys of world and regional economic and social developments continue, year after year, to point to two trends that may, if permitted to go unchecked, be more dangerous in the long run than the conflicts that so monopolize our attention today. One of these is the fact that the population has been increasing faster than production, especially in those areas where standards of living are lowest. The other is the manner in which standards of living in those same areas are still lagging far behind those of the more economically advanced regions. It seems clear that no attack on these trends can be successful without a combination of measures of an order of magnitude far beyond what has so far been undertaken. [77]

❰ The search for peaceful settlements, for collective security and for ultimate disarmament . . . has to be based upon an orderly and steady advance toward higher living standards for all peoples. These standards, in turn, will be unattainable unless world productivity and world trade expand at a pace that more than matches the increase in population. [76]

25

Sharing

"*The obligation of all of us is inescapable. It is to raise the living standards for that two-thirds of humanity who live close to the level of starvation, or below it.*" So said Hammarskjöld at the University of Lund in 1959. He was concerned, however, as well he might be, about the ethics of giving. "*It may be more difficult to receive assistance than to give it,*" he quoted. In India he reminded his audience, "*What you do to help your neighbor, you should do privately and not in the open.*"

Assistance is not a gift from one to another, but a sharing, he said. Sharing "*is a must in our world. It is not in the spirit of sharing if the country which gives wants the gift written on its flag, or if the country which receives has to be constantly reminded of the fact.*"

His preference was for multilateral assistance rather than bi-lateral, with all financial and technical aid channeled through the international body of which both the donors and the receivers are members. "*Only if the receiving country feels that sharing is an act of solidarity within an Organization in which it has equal rights with the donors can the transaction take place with good results psychologically, politically, and economically.*"

Most money given to countries needing assistance comes from the big powers or from big power blocs. Hammarskjöld thought that even small amounts of money, channeled through the United

Nations with no suspicion of strings attached, could help considerably in getting a new nation on its feet.

❡ Through various developments which are familiar to all, world solidarity has, so to say, been forced upon us. This is no longer a free choice of enlightened spirits; it is something which those whose temperament leads them in the direction of isolationism have also to accept. In such a world it is impossible to maintain the status of "haves" and "have-nots," just as impossible as it has grown to be inside the national state.

The weakness of one is the weakness of all, and the strength of one—not the military strength, but the real strength, the economic and social strength, the happiness of the people—is indirectly the strength of all. [8]

❡ What is international aid? . . . It is definitely, as I see it, not the handing out from the haves to the have nots. We live in a world of shared responsibility, in a world with very great unity of fate and destiny, and for that reason I used . . . the term "sharing" (sharing as opposed to handing out). That is the basic philosophy as I see it. It is sharing in a world of joint responsibility; the sharing of knowledge and sharing of resources. [4]

❡ We have in the United Nations no world government, no world parliament, but an organ through which the various states and governments can give expression to their views on this problem of sharing—and an organ which provides the technical instruments for the administration of such sharing.

There is in one of the Christian texts a statement which I think reflects ideas common to all philosophies and all great religions. I refer to the famous words of Saint Paul about the need for faith, hope, and charity and I should like to try to define in those terms.

It is also an instrument for action inspired by hope, and in many corners of the world it stands as a framework for acts of charity. Now, I want to be very clear from the very beginning, so that nobody, when I use the word "charity," misunderstands it. I mean it in the original sense as something a brother does for a brother, not as a handing-out operation with the benevolence of the "haves" in relation to the "have-nots." I mean charity in the sense of mutual cooperation in a well-understood common interest. [8]

⟨ There is the true spirit of cooperation, where we are helping and our help is accepted with an understanding of what it is: a sharing—I repeat the words "a sharing"—of experiences, in which our representatives are your servants during their time in Burma. They are your servants for the time that it will take you to develop experts, people with the broad knowledge needed in all the various professions so that you can take over completely. When that time comes, our people will have fulfilled their mission as your collaborators, and we will follow your future effort with all the sympathy which one has for such efforts in a family or among brothers.

If I have talked too much, you must excuse me—because, as you know, there is an expression in the European scripts that the heart speaks of that of which it is full. [67]

26

Specialized Agencies

To create conditions of stability and well-being "which are necessary for peaceful and friendly relations among nations," the Charter calls for the solution of international economic, social, health, and related problems, and the observance of human rights. The organizations working to this end are called specialized agencies. Their mission is to eradicate the causes that lead to war.

The United Nations has more than fourteen such agencies. They are autonomous within their own sphere but work under the authority of the Economic and Social Council, the final responsibility belonging to the General Assembly.

Hammarskjöld had high praise for the agencies, but he nevertheless expressed the fear that their work was too loosely integrated, and he deplored the proliferation of new agencies, commissions, committees, subcommittees, and so forth, as new fields of activity opened up. In 1960 he told the Chicago University Law School that unless better correlation could be developed, "We may come to face a situation where the very growth of the framework for international cooperation tends to lead to an ultimate weakening. If I am permitted . . . a parallel with biological developments, it is as if we were to permit the growth of a tree to be weakened by the development of too many branches, finally sapping its strength so that it breaks down under its own weight."

He saw also a risk in combining too many tasks within the same organization. "No leaders of such an organization can have the capacity to give satisfactory leadership over ever-expanding areas. We must seek the optimum balance between a system with a large number of autonomous bodies and a system with strong concentration of tasks within a lesser number of organizations."

❲ Policies of growth, international trade and aid, the flow of private capital, although they are far from exhausting the list of responsibilities of the United Nations and the specialized agencies in the economic and social field, are all important topics on which a greater measure of understanding appears at once desirable and, in varying degree, possible. They are important in their own right, in terms of human welfare. They are also related to the other, and major, objective and criterion of United Nations action, the preservation of peace. [51]

❲ The United Nations Children's Fund is joining this year with the World Health Organization in a world-wide campaign to aid governments in achieving the eradication of malaria. This new project is the latest in a series which have helped over 80 million children and their mothers since the Children's Fund was established: in campaigns against tuberculosis, yaws, trachoma, and leprosy; in the extension of elementary maternal and child welfare services to rural areas; and in improving the nutrition of children in under-developed areas. I am sure that governments share with me in recognizing the value and fitness of this United Nations program for the "succeeding generations" of which the Charter speaks, and that they will continue to give it their support. [78]

❲ One matter of interest . . . is a further development of cooperation among the various specialized agencies within the United Nations family. Only by such means can the full effect of a joint and concerted effort of all the agencies be realized. For the same reason, further efforts should be made inside the United Nations itself to concentrate available resources on the main aims of the

Organization and to coordinate activities in the various spheres so that they will mutually support each other. These viewpoints have guided me in attempts to strengthen the ties with the specialized agencies and to increase the efficiency of the Secretariat itself. [77]

⟨ In the vastness of the Congo where so much movement depends on air services, everything would have been grounded . . . but for the air traffic control, the radio and navigation aids, the weather forecasting and telecommunications provided by the International Civil Aviation Organization, the International Telecommunication Union, and the World Meteorological Organization.

International Labor Office programs are dealing with a number of crucial labor and social security fields. Hospitals, abandoned by their medical staff, have been quickly restored . . . and the elementary health services have been maintained by the World Health Organization. Plans and actions for the reopening of schools and the organization of secondary and technical education have largely depended on the activities of the United Nations Educational, Scientific and Cultural Organization. Plans for maintaining agricultural services are being developed through the Food and Agricultural Organization.

All these vitally essential services are rendered under the United Nations flag. [70]

⟨ I think that all those who will take the trouble to reread the Charter and examine the work of the United Nations and the specialized agencies would agree that the United Nations is "in tune" with the basic movements of our time in their positive and constructive manifestations. All its pledges and all its work are in the direction of peaceful progress toward greater social justice within nations and greater political and economic equality and justice between nations. [9]

27

Technical Assistance

The United Nations, together with a number of intergovernmental agencies, provides a way of helping countries to help themselves. Experts in every field—agriculture, engineering, public health, education, and so on—drawn from many nations go to less developed countries and share with them their technical skills.

The technical assistance programs are financed from the regular budget of the United Nations, but an expanded program called the Special Fund, financed by voluntary contributions also exists. It is not a lending institution. Its purpose instead is to finance surveys of a country's resources and to organize educational and training programs. By bringing out the potentialities of a certain nation or area, it makes capital investment more and more attractive, effective, and safe.

A budget of $100 million, to be provided by voluntary contributions, was called for, but individual pledges remained below this total. "Such are, of course, the hazards of voluntary programs," noted Hammarskjöld in a melancholy mood.

He realized that the United Nations Technical Assistance Program, with its limited resources, was no match for a program sponsored by a great power. However, countries accepting assistance from great powers too often find that it comes with strings attached. Hammarskjöld was therefore a zealous supporter of assistance *given through "a universal agency of equal nations where the distinction between donors and receivers tends to dissolve itself."*

In May 1956, in an address at McGill University in Montreal, he proposed a new and imaginative form of technical assistance, called OPEX, its name derived from "Operational and Executive Personnel." Most of the less developed countries suffer from a severe shortage of administrators and civil servants. Under Hammarskjöld's program, the United Nations was to provide trained international officials who would go to the under-developed areas not as advisers, but as employees of the government receiving the assistance, and stay there until local personnel could be trained to take over their duties.

When the program began in 1959, twenty-five OPEX experts were appointed. By 1961, when Hammarskjöld died, their number had increased to eighty-one.

❲ The technical assistance program of the United Nations can realize its promise only to the extent that it can be planned and administered on a long-range basis; and the economic importance of this vital program merits new efforts to achieve these results. [78]

❲ Not only do all participating Member countries share in the responsibilities of over-all direction and control, whether they give or receive aid, but the less developed countries receiving assistance also give aid in those special skills that are found to be of value to other under-developed nations. Thus, the United Nations program of technical assistance is assuming more and more the aspect of a truly cooperative enterprise of mutual aid in the sharing of skills in which nations from all parts of the world and in every stage of economic and social development have something to contribute as well as to receive. [76]

❲ Basic to the United Nations approach to economic and technical assistance is the principle, under all circumstances, that, although the Organization has to follow its own rules and maintain its own independence, its services are exclusively designed to meet the wishes of the recipient government, without the possibility of any ulterior motives and free from the risk of any possible influence on the national or international policies of that government. [19]

¶ In the case of a great power, ... it is difficult to avoid giving a political overtone to its technical assistance, even though all such conditions may be expressly waived. The beneficiary tends to feel his economic dependence as a political liability. Political considerations apart, the fact remains that the beneficiary country —often a newcomer on the world scene—feels the burden of maintaining relations of indebtedness and gratitude to another country.

Because of these political and psychological factors, multilateral forms of assistance have emerged as superior to the bilateral ones in important respects. If aid is channeled from the giver country to the beneficiary country through the United Nations or one of the specialized agencies within the United Nations framework, a political accent is avoided and psychological pressure is eased in other ways at the same time.

It is not my contention that the multilateral form should supplant the bilateral one. Both are needed. What I want to stress is that bilateral forms are insufficient and face difficulties which make it urgent to pursue the multilateral course further and fully utilize its potentialities. This focuses attention from another side upon the question of the necessity of the United Nations. [6]

¶ If multilateral assistance cannot be provided, it is difficult to go to a country and request, for this or that political reason, that they should not ask for, or receive bilateral assistance which is badly needed—and offered. [68]

❲ I guess that aid through the United Nations to countries will always be only a fraction of aid received from Big Powers or from power blocs, but that does not mean that it cannot be decisive. It depends entirely on where we put it in and under what kind of leadership. Eight hundred thousand dollars does not mean the same as 80 million dollars from the point of view of investment, but from the point of view of what I call moral support it may be used in such a way as to carry greater weight.

It is infinitely easier to receive financial assistance and technical assistance by experts and so on through an international body than on a bilateral basis, and it is infinitely easier for them to receive it through an international body of which they are themselves members than through any other international body of which they are not members.

The United Nations, for these reasons, without pushing, without, so to say, becoming a party in their development, can through proper means, even on the basis of fairly small amounts of money, come in to the picture in such a way as to help considerably in the framing of their political life after independence and in the building up of the national state. [46]

❲ In the long run we all must hope for the situation wherein the political side can go a little bit backwards and in which economic and social activities will find foremost position. That situation can only be brought about when the United Nations can no longer be regarded as a kind of political watch dog, but primarily as a center of self-help and an organ for providing technical assistance. [63]

❲ In the present world situation, we have had a tendency to give much attention to the need for a wider movement of capital to areas in need of economic development. We are right in doing so. The needs are enormous. But even more important than the money are the skills. . . . Fundamentally, man is the key to our problems, not money. Funds are valuable only when used by trained, experienced and devoted men and women. Such people, on the other hand, can work miracles even with small resources and draw wealth out of a barren land. [30]

❨ The capacity of a country to absorb large-scale economic assistance or to make the best use of its domestic resources is in no small measure determined by its administrative arrangements.

Nations emerging from long foreign rule generally lack an independent administrative tradition and a social structure within which it is easy to build up a class of national administrators. This is a major problem not only for such nations, but also for many other countries which seek to achieve a major economic and social reconstruction and to use international economic assistance in the best possible way for this end. [31]

❨ It will take many of the new countries twenty to thirty years to train enough administrators. If they are to carry out their development plans, what are they to do in the meantime? They do not want to be directly dependent on other nations. But the main sources from which they can draw trained manpower for administration are the industrially advanced countries.

I am sure there are many thousands of able men and women who would be glad to dedicate part or all of their lives to such a service. And I am equally sure of the need for their service and of the welcome they would receive if they went under the auspices of the World Organization. [13]

After an extensive visit to the Middle East and Asia in 1956,

Hammarskjöld gave a press conference at which he uttered what was for him an unusually emotional statement:

❪ I remember very many personalities and very many situations. I remember the enthusiasm, the pure enthusiasm, of the young people in the collectives in Israel. I remember an old woman quite alone in a refugee camp in Beirut, scared of people, tired. I remember the young workers in an Indian village, at the end of a long day, breaking out in a dance with a zest of life going far beyond anything I have ever seen. I remember the old women in the Peace Pagoda at Rangoon, praying for peace with flowers in their hands—poor, poor people who did not know much about the ways of this world, but knew that short of peace there was no future for them. That is the human side.

Close to the human side is what I would call the economic and social aspect of life in these various member countries. All of us are very much aware of the plight and problem of the refugees . . . the poverty of the squatters in those areas of the world where great migrations have taken place and where, so far, the governments have not been in a position to provide adequate housing. I do not want to mention any specific place; I saw several places, in fact. But the experience was always one and the same: the enormity of the task which all responsible governments in the world have before them, the enormity of the plight of those people who have been thrown around in the world owing to political circumstances over which they have had no control.

There are, however, positive sides to this field, too. There are the very progressive, the very fne plans for economic development which one finds in several countries—plans tackled with wisdom, energy and very great courage. Again, I should not like to mention any specific country; I saw examples in several places. And these are not empty programs; these are programs involving the mere rustling of paper; there are programs with a very strong human content. . . . These are the places where one sees an economic revolution from the grass roots, an economic revolution lifting a people out from the middle ages, not into our world of today with fine, modern tools, but at least into a world where they have a possibility of developing free, individual lives.

Whether it is a question of politicians and governments or a question of the sample man—the famous man in the street—the United Nations is in these parts of the world very much more than we perhaps always realize here at Headquarters. [36]

28

Regional Organizations

Nothing in the United Nations Charter precludes the existence of regional arrangements to achieve the peaceful settlements of local disputes—bodies similar to the Organization of the American States (OAS). In fact the Security Council is enjoined to encourage such organizations. Europe has its Common Market; the Communist nations have their COMECON (Council of Mutual Assistance and Cooperation); and there are politico-military organizations such as NATO, the Warsaw Pact, and the Arab League.

Ideally these alliances should form stepping-stones toward broader unity. However, they have not, and furthermore they are not particularly unified within themselves. There is friction within NATO, the Warsaw Pact, the Common Market, and COMECON; the Arab League is a veritable squabbling league. The germ of conflict lives in them, for they are all pitted against somebody or against each other.

Hammarskjöld, while obliged under the Charter to support such arrangements, nevertheless was alive to their trouble-making potentialities, and he was far more satisfied with the regional economic organizations maintained by the United Nations, such as the Economic Commissions for Europe, Latin America, Africa, Asia, and the Far East. By facilitating commerce and opening up new means of communication, these organizations are doing an excellent job, especially in Africa and Latin America. They are not confined to political and ideological boundaries. Their work is in the spirit of the Charter, is done on behalf of their members, and is pitted against none.

〔 It is known that Sir Winston Churchill, in his time, advocated an approach to the building of a world community through the creation of regional organizations as stepping-stones to more highly developed forms of international coexistence or cooperation. We see instead the advance being made in part only through regional arrangements, but in part—and mainly—independently of such arrangements and directly on the basis of universality. If Sir Winston's line had been followed, it would, with my terminology, have meant that regional organizations step by step would have developed a basic institutional pattern for universal coexistence by which, later on, a push forward, on the universal level, could have been tried in the direction of a constitutional pattern.

If we accept the interpretation given here to the European community and the French-African community, the United Nations could, in a similar sense, be called a "community," although of a universal character.

With the recent creation of the European Common Market of six nations, the Coal and Steel Community, and similar bodies, a decisive step has been taken in the further development of this institutional framework. In fact, by these actions the system has been pushed beyond the border of institutional arrangements and has come to include some initial constitutional elements.

The institutional evolution in Europe has brought us a step in the direction of a true constitutional framework for cooperation which, through experimental stages of a confederal nature, may finally lead to some kind of federal system or even stronger forms of association. [9]

〔 At the regional level . . . many countries are acting to secure the benefits that may come from the lowering of trade barriers and increasing the degree of economic integration. The time has perhaps come when the United Nations should consider whether concerted action for the expansion of international markets for exports of under-developed countries might not bear similar fruit. [51]

⟨ The United Nations can welcome regional arrangements among neighboring or like-minded countries. As long as such arrangements are so designed as to reinforce rather than to supplant the common effort toward establishing conditions of economic and social progress, they have an important role to play. A real danger arises, however, when such regional arrangements are so envisaged as to make them fall into the sphere of bloc conflict. In that case, efforts which properly should embody and be supported by a common interest may instead lead to a weakening of the uniting force of that interest and aggravate the split. [18]

⟨ The governments can no longer succeed in promoting and protecting the peace, security, and well-being of their peoples by national and regional efforts alone. [76]

29

Do We Need the United Nations?

It worried Hammarskjöld that such a question could be asked, and he answered it again and again, addressing his remarks to the doubters and the cynics; to those impatient with slow development and to those who rejected without trying to understand. The United Nations needs such explanation because it has no historic precedent and its machinery remains something of a mystery. Certainly the United Nations is still too weak to provide the security envisioned in the Charter, but it is strong enough and alive enough, Hammarskjöld thought, to point the direction where solutions must be sought. "The Organization may look to many like a preacher who cannot impose the law he states or realize the gospel he interprets. . . . But the effort to implement an ideal does not prove that the ideal is wrong."

There must be a stage, he felt, at the beginning of any great change in human society, of frailty or seeming inconsistency. The United Nations is only a first approximation of what we need and what one day must come about. In the meantime, all its pledges, all its work, are in the direction of peaceful progress toward greater social justice within nations and greater political and economic equality among nations.

"The United Nations is and should be," he told the American Jewish Committee in 1957, "a living, evolving, experimental insti-

*tution. If it should ever cease to be, it should be revolutionized or
set aside for a new approach."*

❪ Look anywhere in the world today. Is there any solution in
sight except peacefully negotiated agreements? Granted that at a
given moment the prospects for such agreements seem dim indeed. What is the alternative? Only the attempt to establish "one
world" by force of arms. And that is no alternative. Such an
attempt would lead to a catastrophe just as fatal to the presumed
victor as to the vanquished. [23]

❪ As an instrument for conciliation, the United Nations provides
a forum which should serve the Members less for the voicing of
complaints and more for the presentation of proposals furthering
the common end. The Organization can grow in influence only
insofar as the peoples of the world feel that what is brought out
in its conference rooms represents an expression of the constructive will of the Member nations to put the common international interest before national demands. [76]

❪ We need the Organization in the present situation for the
negotiating possibilities it opens up. We need it as an executive
organ. We need it for the constructive additions it offers in international attempts to resolve conflicts of interest. And we need it
as a foundation and a framework for arduous and time-consuming
attempts to find forms in which an extra-national—or perhaps
even supra-national—influence may be brought to bear in the
prevention of future conflicts. [10]

❪ It is quite true that the United Nations cannot assure even-
handed justice in the settlement of disputes, mainly because it
does not have power to enforce its recommendations. But what
the United Nations can do, if wisely used, is to help us to move
forward in the direction of that goal. [13]

⟪ A failure to gain respect for decisions or actions of the Organization within the terms of the Charter is often called a failure for the Organization. It would seem more correct to regard it as a failure of the world community, through its Member nations and in particular those most directly concerned, to cooperate in order, step by step, to make the Charter a living reality in practical political action as it is already in law. [19]

⟪ I believe, and many believe with me, that this Organization in all its frailty represents the sole approach which may give us a chance to reduce the risk that the constant frictions—large and small—which characterize the life of our present-day world build up to a tension easily triggered into a clash in which we would all be engulfed. I also believe that it is essential for the growth of a human society in which the dignity of the human being will be respected that every effort is made to make this step in the direction of an organized world community of success. [54]

⟪ It is impossible to say that the Organization as such solved difficult problems but it is possible to say that development has been more orderly, quicker, and in a more sound, healthy, constructive direction than would have been the case if the negotiations had been conducted otherwise. [63]

⟪ I personally believe that, just as negotiation keeps people from shooting, in the same way reasonable progress toward a goal keeps people from rushing into a conflict because they cannot get everything at once or cannot get it in just the form that they would like. [36]

⟪ In our day, too, we often hear it said that the United Nations has succeeded here, or has failed there. What do we mean? Do we refer to the purposes of the Charter? They are expressions of universally shared ideals which cannot fail us, though we, alas, often fail them. Or do we think of the institutions of the United Nations? They are our tools. We fashioned them. We use them. It is our responsibility to remedy any flaws there may be in them. It is our responsibility to correct any failures in our use of them. And we must expect the responsibility for remedying the flaws and correcting the failures to go on and on, as long as human beings are imperfect and human institutions likewise. [31]

❨ The Charter, read as a whole, does not endow the United Nations with any of the attributes of a super-State or of a body active outside the framework of decisions of Member governments. The United Nations is, rather, an instrument for negotiation among, and to some extent for, governments. It is also an instrument added to the time-honored means of diplomacy for concerting action by governments in support of the goals of the Charter. This is the role the Organization has played, sometimes successfully, sometimes with disappointing setbacks, throughout its life. [38]

❨ If you permit me a somewhat literary association, one is rather tempted to quote Shelley when he says, if I remember correctly, that one should "hope 'til Hope creates from its own wreck the thing it contemplates."* I would like to make that the motto in quite a few United Nations operations and also for a few operations outside the United Nations, including their talks. [61]

❨ In the diplomacy of World Organization the quiet work of preparing the ground, of accommodation of interest and viewpoint, of conciliation and mediation, all that goes into the winning of consent to agreed solutions and common programs, this forms a basis upon which the United Nations can become an increasingly influential and effective force to aid the governments in pursuit of the goals of the Charter. [37]

---

*Prometheus Unbound; the reference is to the collapsed French-Algerian peace talks in Milan.

(No matter how deep the shadows may be, how sharp the conflicts, how tense the mistrust reflected in what is said and done
in our world of today as reflected in this hall and in this house,
we are not permitted to forget that we have too much in common,
too great a sharing of interests and too much that we might lose
together, for ourselves and for succeeding generations, ever to
weaken in our efforts to surmount the difficulties and not to turn
the simple human values, which are our common heritage, into
the firm foundation on which we may unite our strength and
live together in peace. [51]

(The United Nations is a positive response by the world community to the fundamental needs of our time. Its record should
be judged against this background. Its efforts are significant insofar as they show the growing maturity of the Organization as
an instrument by means of which the nations can solve conflicts
threatening the natural evolution of the world community. They
are significant insofar as they represent successful steps by that
community in the direction indicated by the underlying trends in
social and international development. This perspective should
help to put the Organization in its proper light as an expression
of the will of the peoples to achieve cooperation in a guided development toward social and international justice as a basis of
social and international peace.

The work of the United Nations should always be viewed as
a continuing process over a long period of time in which there
is constant change and development. It is difficult to measure the
significance of results in the perspective of any single year. Often
the unspectacular or the unnoticed may prove to be a significant
forward step on the long road toward peace in a world of organized cooperation and of more equal partnership among the
nations.

The pursuit of peace and progress cannot end in a few years
in either victory or defeat. The pursuit of peace and progress,

with its trials and its errors, its successes and its setbacks, can never be relaxed and never abandoned.

Two fundamental trends in human society are apparent which must determine the long-term direction of our efforts. One of the trends is directed toward wider social justice and equality for individuals. The other is directed toward equality and justice between nations, politically but also in the economic and social sense. [76]

❨ At present, the Organization is severely handicapped by the fact that it has to function in a world where the necessity of coexistence is as yet not fully recognized. But this is, in itself, an additional and compelling reason for doing everything possible to strengthen the United Nations. The increasing danger of destruction will sooner or later force us out of a system of balance of power into a system of true and universal international cooperation. [77]

❨ We may believe that the United Nations needs basic reforms. We may even share the view held by some that its task ultimately will have to be taken over by a body with a different structure. However, we cannot doubt that the main direction of the work of the United Nations, as determined by the purposes and principles of the Charter, indicates the path which the world must follow in order to preserve the achievements of the past and to lay a basis for a happier future. [15]

❨ What is needed is not a revision of the Charter. What is needed is a revision of the world situation. [5]

30

World Government

As Hammarskjöld exercised even more executive power and frequently used such expressions as "world order," "international coexistence," and "supranational executive organ," fear germinated in some hearts that he was purposefully leading the Organization toward world government or some sort of world federation. Andrei Gromyko, taking the opportunity to voice these fears before the General Assembly at a time when the Secretary-General was under fire for his handling of the Congo situation, said, "If Hammarskjöld is allowed to follow this course, he may assume himself to be the Prime Minister of a World Government."

Hammarskjöld's actual point of view emerges clearly from his speeches and writings. He did not believe in any system imposed from without or from above; he believed in one which grew out of and progressed step by step with organized world society. "No one can foresee with certainty what will emerge from the give and take of forces at work in any age. History often seems to run its course beyond the reach of any man or nation." Creative evolution was the dynamic factor, and he had faith in its ultimate result. Many of his statements suggest that he shared Leo Frobenius' theory that human societies undergo an organic development similar to that which can be observed in the lives of plants, animals, and men: a progress from immaturity through the confusion of adolescence to the integrated adult state. He seemed also to subscribe to the Lamarckian theory of evolution which holds that a giraffe has a long neck not only because natural selection has favored giraffes who could reach the leaves on the top of the trees, but also because giraffes wanted to have long necks. "We can influence the development of the world from within," said Hammarskjöld, "as a spiritual thing."

He commented upon Christ's injunction in the Sermon on the Mount: "Take therefore no thought for the morrow, for the morrow shall take thought for the things of itself. Sufficient unto the day is the evil thereof." These words, he said, certainly do not mean that we should act thoughtlessly, without responsible consideration of future consequences: "But they mean that our work for peace should be pursued with the patience of one who has no anxiety about results, acting in the calm self-surrender of faith."

A pragmatist but not a conformist, Hammarskjöld took care of the evil of the day with an eye on the future. He was a pragmatist with a vision.

❲ It is impossible for anyone to say where the international community is heading and how the United Nations will change in the further course of evolution of international politics. But it can safely be said that international cooperation will become increasingly essential for the maintenance of peace, progress, and international justice. [18]

❲ Nations and groups of nations will never again be able to live and to arrogate judgment unto themselves in international affairs in ways which once were a matter of course. [38]

❲ We undoubtedly need world organization, but we are far from ripe for world government. Indeed, even modest attempts at regional "integration" have met with considerable difficulties, not because of any superstitious respect for national sovereignty, but because the peoples want to know in whose hands they put their fate, if they are to surrender part of their self-determination as nations. Further: how often have we not seen those who most eagerly plead for integration among other countries themselves shrink back from even the slightest discipline of their own sovereign rights? [27]

⟨ It is often said that the solution of the problem of international coexistence must be world federation. Unfortunately, it is necessary to learn to crawl before one can walk. And it is rather risky to refuse to move at all just because one has not learned how to walk. [7]

⟨ Those who advocate world government, and this or that special form of world federalism, often present challenging theories and ideas, but we, like our ancestors, can only press against the receding wall which hides the future. It is by such efforts, pursued to the best of our ability, more than by the construction of ideal patterns to be imposed upon society, that we lay the basis and pave the way for the society of the future. [9]

⟨ Some are tempted to seek a solution in constitutional reform which would turn the United Nations into a world authority enforcing the law upon the nations. While respecting the goal of those who advocate such a course, most of us would agree that the political realities with which we live, rooted as they are deep in the disparate histories and cultures of many peoples, make this course impracticable in the foreseeable future.

At this stage of human history, world organization has become necessary. The forces at work have also set the limits within which the power of world organization can develop at each step and beyond which progress, when the balance of forces so permits, will be possible only by processes of organic growth in the system of custom and law prevailing in the society of nations. [13]

⟦ Undoubtedly, there are some who still dislike the idea of a group of political representatives from countries far from the storm center passing judgment on the actors in the drama and making recommendations for a solution of conflicts. But is that not a true expression of a very real interdependence, where aggression in Korea may forebode dangers to a country at the other end of the globe? [24]

⟦ We live in a period of fundamental and rapid changes in the relationship of nations and peoples having differing cultures and social systems. The new age that is emerging is an age of promise. It could also become one disaster. We are seeking to cope with world issues of great difficulty but equally of high challenge. The hope of finding peaceful, just, and constructive solutions of these issues rests upon our ability to foster the growth of understanding, cooperation, and mutual accommodation of interests among all the nations. [32]

⟦ The spirit and practice of world community must first gain in strength and custom by processes of organic growth. It is to the helping along of these processes of growth that we should devote all our ingenuity and our effort. To the extent that we are able to increase the weight of the common interest as against the weight of special interests, and therefore of the power of the whole community to guide the course of events, we shall be approaching that much nearer to the goal. [31]

⟦ Only those who do not want to see can deny that we are moving these days in the direction of a new community of nations, however far we may be from its full realization, however often we may seem to have chosen the wrong path, however numerous the setbacks and disappointments have been. Could it be otherwise, when no other road appears open out of the dangers a new era has created? [39]

⟦ Each conquest of new ground for diplomatic activity and international cooperation is a lasting gain for the future. [7]

❡ Those are lost who permit defeats to scare them back to a starting point of narrow nationalism. Those are lost who are so scared by a defeat as to despair about the future. [1]

❡ Where our predecessors dreamt of a new heaven, our greatest hope is that we may be permitted to save the old earth. Beyond that hope, however, are now rallied all peoples of the world. [5]

❡ I do not think that there is anything automatic in progress. I do not think that there is anything we get for nothing in success. But I do believe firmly that here in this room, around this Organization, in this city, in this country, in the world, there are enough people who are solidly engaged in this fight and who are strong enough and dedicated enough to guarantee its success.

It is in a sense a switch from the atmosphere of pre-1914 to what I believe is the atmosphere of our generation in this time— a switch from the, so to say, mechanical optimism of previous generations to what I might call the fighting optimism of this present generation. We have learned it the hard way, and we will certainly have to learn it again and again and again.

I cannot belong to or join with those who believe in our movement toward catastrophe. I believe in growth, a growth to which we have a responsibility to add our few fractions of an inch. [40]

❡ I believe that the hope of a world of peace and order, inspired by respect for man, has never ceased to agitate the minds of men. I believe that it accounts for the great and noble human spirit behind the ravaged exterior of a history whose self-inflicted wounds have become more and more atrocious. And I believe that at the point we have now reached in our technical development, our creed may gain new possibilities to shape history.

It is natural that this new situation should provoke a resistance, inspired by the fear that our own country and our own private world might find itself submerged in some global development. And so we find people trying to find ways to isolate themselves from general trends and to build up closed, protected units. We can understand or even sympathize with such a reaction, but we must recognize that if it represents a resistance to change, it is doomed to failure. Such self-sought isolation may persevere for some time. It will not endure forever, and the longer the change is resisted and adjustment shirked, the more violent will be the final reaction when the walls collapse. [27]

⟨ Although justice requires that we recognize the heritage, it would, however, be unjust to belittle the significance of the act through which ideas break through the barriers and become an active factor in the life of the community. [43]

⟨ The revolutionary events we witness have led many into a defeatism which, although unspoken, is revealed by its inseparable companions: fatigue, bitterness, and sterile self-assertion.

There are good reasons, and good chances, to offer resistance to such a situation. The old is not so rotten, nor the new so immature, as many seem to think. [39]

⟨ Perhaps a future generation, which knows the outcome of our present efforts, will look at them with some irony. They will see where we fumbled and they will find it difficult to understand why we did not see the direction more clearly and work more consistently toward the target it indicates. So it will always be, but let us hope that they will not find any reason to criticize us because of a lack of that combination of steadfastness of purpose and flexibility of approach which alone can guarantee that the possibilities which we are exploring will have been tested to the full. [9]

⟨ The future will be all right because there will always be enough people to fight for a decent future. [40]

⟨ The United Nations is only a first approximation to the world order which we need and which one day must be brought about. [43]

⟨ To turn aside from the United Nations now because it cannot be transformed into a world authority enforcing the law upon the nations would be to erase all the steady, though slow and painful advances that have been made and to close the door to hopes for the future of world society, toward which present efforts and experiences should be at least a modest stepping-stone. [38]

⟨ What seems imperative is to push forward institutionally and, eventually, constitutionally all along the line, guided by current needs and experiences, without preconceived ideas of the ultimate form. [9]

31

Creative Evolution

Philosophers in our day usually live in the back streets of university towns, and their abstract notions are rarely brought to bear upon our understanding of practical affairs, as they were in the days of the ancient Greeks. Hammarskjöld was that rare public figure, Plato's "philosopher king," aware of the essential unity of science, art, religion, philosophy, and human institutions, and always alert for lessons to be learned from any field of thought which could be applied to politics.

Hammarskjöld borrowed the term coined by the French Philosopher Henri Bergson, "creative evolution," to denote free and continuous development feeding on an accumulation of vital powers and bringing about the inventiveness of life and mind. Life is a "continual elaboration of the absolutely new," the opposite of inertia and the opposite of accident. There is a direction in growth which is built-in.

Hammarskjöld used this theory as a key to the understanding of the organic development of human institutions.

❪ It is difficult to see how a leap from today's chaotic and disjointed world to something approaching a world federation is to come about. To attain such a goal, elements of organic growth are required. We must serve our apprenticeship and at every stage try to develop the forms of international coexistence as far as is possible at the moment, if we are to be justified in hoping some day to realize the more radical solutions which the situation may seem to call for. We must, for instance, feel our way along the road of majority voting and get to know its political and psychological possibilities and difficulties in international life. We shall have to create a corps of administrators and diplomats who know, from within, the questions facing an international organization with political tasks. For such a development, the United Nations offers a framework which appears as good as the world situation permits at present. [6]

⟨ It is essential for the growth of human society in which the dignity of the human being will be respected that every effort be made to make this step [the United Nations] in the direction of an organized world community a success. [54]

⟨ Two of our most common human failings, indeed, seem to be our disrespect for the slow processes of time and our tendency to shift responsibility from ourselves to our institutions. It is too often our habit to see the goal, to declare it and, in declaring it, to assume that we shall automatically achieve it. This leads us to confuse ends with means, to label as failure what is in fact a historic step forward, and in general to mistake the lesser for the greater thing. [31]

⟨ We all have a tendency to regard the situation as it exists at any single moment as a lasting one, forgetting that we ourselves and the societies which we form are all subject to the law of change. Those people and nations which are to live together in the future, if we succeed in overcoming the immediate risks of war, will not be of the same generation as those who do not see any possibility of living together as they are now and as conditions are today. [23]

◖ In every society there is a tendency, as time passes, to lose dynamism and to seek protection behind time-honored formulae, protection against the law of change which is basic to all growth. [30]

◖ I believe it is useful, in the discussion of the development of human society, be it national or international, to keep in mind this sociological perspective taken over from theories of biological evolution. It is a perspective which helps us to a more realistic appraisal of what it is we have achieved and what it is we are trying to do, as well as of the scope and significance of our failure and our successes.

However primitive a basic institutional pattern may be, it carries within it seeds for the growth of higher social organisms, covering wider areas and groups of people. [9]

◖ The United Nations, as a living organism, has the necessary scope for a continuous adaptation of its constitutional life to the needs. [17]

◖ We are all human beings and we were meant to make the United Nations a thing of perfection. We are not ripe for that kind of perfection yet, but I must say what I have said before: if the elephant walks, and walks in the right direction, we should not be impatient. It does not move too quickly, and we shall certainly arrive at a goal. [4]

◖ Conflicts, not only in human life, but also in the life of nations, are often never resolved, but simply outgrown. [23]

◖ Working at the edge of the development of human society is to work on the brink of the unknown. Much of what is done will one day prove to have been of little avail. That is no excuse for the failure to act in accordance with our best understanding, in recognition of its limits but with faith in the ultimate result of the creative evolution in which it is our privilege to cooperate. [9]

[Asked at a press conference to be specific about what he meant by the phrase "the edge of the development of human society," Hammarskjöld commented:]

⟨ Of course we are working on the brink of the unknown because we have no idea as to what the international society of tomorrow will be. We can only do what we can now to find solutions in a pragmatic sense to the problems as they arise, trying to keep the sense of direction, and then we will see later on what comes out of it.

You may find a further clue . . . in the final words where I happened to use the Bergsonian term "creative evolution." [2]

⟨ In us the creative instinct became will. In order to grow beautifully like a tree, we have to attain a peaceful self-unity in which the creative will is re-transformed into instinct. [83]

32

The Rule of Law

A code of law implies the existence of individuals and groups of individuals who are inclined to submit to it. In a world composed of independent nation states which are far from anxious to accept any limitation on their freedom of action, the development of international law is slow. The International Court of Justic at The Hague was set up before the First World War for the peaceful settlement of disputes; but its work is still at an early stage of development.

Hammarskjöld pleaded with the Member Nations to use the facilities of the Court more frequently than they do; he thought that a number of controveries dragging on between governments, a continuing source of tension, were suitable for judicial settlement through the Court.

Since no ultimate authority stands behind the Court, the decisions it hands down cannot be enforced. Some say that there is not much point in making a law if enforcement is impossible. Hammarskjöld tried, as usual, to bring a sense of rightness, perhaps conscience, to bear upon the matter. "It should not be forgotten that if a law is the inescapable law of the future, it would be treason not to make it simply because of the difficulties of the present. Indeed, how could it ever become a living reality, if those who are responsible for its development are to succumb to the immediate difficulties?"

*In the introduction to his annual report of 1958–1959, he as-
serted that the acceptance of international law was absolutely
essential to an orderly world of the future. "There is a glimpse
here of a world society where nation states live under the protection of internationalism which gains its strength from the very
logic of justice itself."*

❮ We have to come to realize the significance of economic and
social matters. We have, alas, not been permitted to lose sight of
the significance of pure politics. But I think we have let those
two aspects overshadow a little too much the significance of law.
I would hope that in the next decade governments would support
a stronger development in the field of international law—codification of international law, first of all—and a freer and more
frequent appeal to the International Court of Justice. [8]

❮ One may recognize that the reluctance of governments to submit their controveries to judicial settlement stems in part from
the fragmentary and uncertain character of much of international
law as it now exists. Where wide margins of uncertainty remain
in the law, the tendency to seek a political settlement even in
cases where questions of law lie at the heart of the dispute is
understandable. Yet in the longer view, it is surely in the interest
of all Member States to restrict as much as possible the sphere
where sheer strength is an argument and to extend as widely as
possible the area ruled by considerations of law and justice. In an
interdependent world, a greater degree of authority and effective-
ness in international law will be a safeguard, not a threat, to the
freedom and independence of national States. [78]

❮ The United Nations cannot lay down the laws for life within
any national community. Those laws have to be established in
accordance with the will of the people as expressed in the forms
indicated by their chosen constitution. But just as the United
Nations can promote peace, so it can, in joint deliberations, define

the goals of human rights which should be the laws of the future in every nation. Whatever the distance between these goals and the everyday reality we meet all around the world, it is not vain thus to set the targets as they present themselves to the most mature political thinking of our age. [34]

⟨[The system of international law is still fairly undeveloped and there are wide margins of uncertainty. Why, one may ask, run the risk of a possibly less favorable outcome reached on the basis of law instead of a more advantageous one that might be achieved by skillful negotiation and under the pressure of political arguments. Why? Is not the reason obvious? First of all, is it not in the interest of sound development to restrict as much as possible the arena where strength is an argument and to put as much as possible under the rule of law? [28]

⟨[The development and acceptance of international law impartially administered by judicial tribunals is essential to progress toward a more just and peaceful international order. [17]

⟨[As individuals we know that the law which restrains us likewise protect us. The same holds true in international life. [34]

⟨[We must recognize that the nations have been for the most part slow to submit their juridical disputes to the International Court of Justice and thus to build up a body of decisions respected by the international community. It is also disturbing that the movement to extend and codify international law on crimes against the peace and against humanity, which was so strong at the end of the war and in the first days of the United Nations, has diminished in momentum. [76]

⟨[International law, in spite of the vast literature covering the subject, has on the whole been less favored by serious students than national law.

In fact, international constitutional law is still in an embryonic stage; we are still in transition between institutional systems of international coexistence and constitutional systems of international cooperation.

We have the International Court of Justice as a counterpart to a national judiciary. It would be possible for it to develop into a more important element in the settlement of international conflicts than it now is, were the unfortunate and self-defeating reservations against its jurisdiction made by some Member countries to be withdrawn. [9]

⟨ The defense of international law is a contribution to the effort to guide the general development in such a way that the basic ideals of freedom and justice, which inspire and support our life, are not lost or obscured. Upheld in international life, their victory in national life also will be brought closer.

No organized international development can take place unless it is founded on a respect for international law and an acceptance of the obligations which that law imposes. [76]

⟨ As in national life, the principle of justice—which obviously implies also the principle of objectivity and equity in the consideration of all matters before the General Assembly or the Security Council—must be considered as applicable without distinction or discrimination, with one measure and one standard valid for the strong as well as for the weak. Thus, the demand of the Charter for a rule of law aims at the substitution of right for might and makes of the Organization the natural protector of rights which countries, without it, might find it more difficult to assert and to get respected. [19]

⟨[The United Nations will never grow and prosper in the way we hope for, unless the central role of the judiciary comes to be recognized in the international sphere as fully as it is in national life. [28]

⟨[The growth of international law and jurisdiction is essential, not only as a way to safeguard the nations whose interest may be directly involved, but also as a means to give a solid basis to our efforts to achieve and maintain world peace. In international law expression has been given to ideals which are the result of a long and often painful development of human society. [76]

⟨[The world of order and justice for which we are striving will never be ours unless we are willing to give it the broadest possible and the firmest possible foundation in law. [28]

33

Faith and Order

Hammarskjöld the mystic was quick to grasp the fact that the United Nations, a radical political institution, was finding strong support among churches. He frequently addressed religious groups of all faiths, expressing to them his own unifying mysticism, and directing their attention to the United Nations as an "instrument of faith . . . inspired by what unites and not by what divides the great religions of the world."

The churches, he said, could help to explain what an organization like the United Nations stands for, how its ideals run parallel to the ancient desire of the "common man who wishes to live in peace with his neighbors, with freedom to build his own little world in human dignity." What is required of the governments and peoples represented in the Organization was "renewed faith, a faith renewed every day, expressed in a never-abandoned, every day newly initiated, responsible action for peace."

⟨ Faith and Order. These words could, with only a slight change of sense, serve as a motto also for the United Nations in its international activity. The Organization must be animated by and defend Faith in the dignity and worth of men, born equal. It must serve and strengthen Order as a guarantee for peace, giving to everyone a possibility to live a full life of freedom.

Mustn't we learn to believe that when we give to this work, daily, what it is in our power to give, and when, daily, we meet the demands facing us to all the extent of our ability, this will ultimately lead to a world of greater justice and good will, even if nothing would seem to give us hope of success or even of progress in the right direction.

The Organization and the churches stand side by side as participants in the efforts of all men of good will, irrespective of their creed or form of worship, to establish peace on earth. Problems that worry us in the United Nations must worry you, and achievements which we may be permitted to make will be welcomed by you.

For the Christian faith "the Cross is that place at the center of the world's history . . . where all men and all nations without exception stand revealed as enemies of God . . . and yet where all men stand revealed as beloved of God, precious in God's sight." So understood, the Cross, although it is the unique fact on which the Christian churches base their hope, should not separate those of Christian faith from others but should instead be that element in their lives which enables them to stretch out their hands to peoples of other creeds in the feeling of universal brotherhood which we hope one day to see reflected in a world of nations truly united.

In a televised interview some time ago, a youngster of sixteen asked me with concern why there is no reference to God in the United Nations Charter. In my reply I drew his attention to the Preamble of the Charter where the nations express their "faith in the dignity and worth of the human person" and pledge themselves "to practice tolerance and live together in peace with one another as good neighbors." I felt sure that he saw here an expression of what, in the faith which was his, was recognized as the will of God: that we should love our neighbors as ourselves. He could not expect a document which should serve as a basis for world cooperation to go further in the direction he had in mind. The United Nations must recognize and respect all the different creeds and attitudes represented by its Member nations.

The question and my reply emphasize some basic facts. The United Nations stands outside—necessarily outside—all confessions but it is, nevertheless, an instrument of faith. As such it is inspired by what unites and not by what divides the great religions of the world.

The churches are guardians of and spokesmen for the deepest beliefs and the loftiest dreams of man. The United Nations, on the other hand, is an organization for continuous diplomatic negotiation concerning concrete political issues, providing also for international administrative action in the economic and social fields.

Yet, in spite of all differences in character and responsibility, the churches and the United Nations have an aim in common and a field of action where they work side by side.

In speaking for justice, truth, and trust in public affairs, the churches may be a decisive force for good in international and national political life, without assuming a political role or trying directly to influence political decisions. Can or should the churches go any further? In my view there is one thing they could do. They could help to explain how world affairs are run and what is the responsibility of every one of us. In doing so they could help to explain what an organization like the United Nations stands for: how its ideals run parallel to the very aims and beliefs of the common man who wishes to live in peace with his neighbors, with freedom to build his own little world in human dignity.

The conflicts behind the surface of international—and for that matter also of national—politics, are conflicts whose battlefield always has been, is, and always will be the hearts of men.

A war to be fought in the hearts of men can be waged only by those speaking directly to men. It is here that I see the great, the overwhelming task of the churches and of all men of good will of every creed in the work for peace. Their vital contribution to this work is to fight for an ever wider recognition of their own ideals of justice and truth. [25]

❲ The *Baghavad-Gita* echoes somewhere an experience of all ages and all philosophies in these words: Work with anxiety about results is far inferior to work without such anxiety, in calm self-surrender. These are words of worldly wisdom which we can all share. But they also express a deep faith. We will be happy if we can make that faith ours in all our efforts. [23]

❲ Dejection and despair lead to defeatism—and defeat. [58]

❲ A couple of days ago, in Bangalore, I saw some Indian dances in the Lal Bagh Gardens. One of the dances was based on a poem by Rabindranath Tagore, and, in thanking our hosts, I felt that it was appropriate to quote a few lines of the poem which was presented in the dance. These are the lines:

> Listen to the rumbling of the clouds, oh heart of mine.
> Be brave, break through and leave for the unkown assignation.

I think that these lines, which—at least to me, as a European—seem typical of deep trends of thought in this people, express in a very noble way the attitude we must take to this venture which is the United Nations. We may listen to the rumbling of the clouds, but we can never afford to lose that kind of confidence in ourselves and in the wisdom of man which makes us brave enough to break through and leave—always leave—for the unknown assignation. [8]

❲ The effort to realize, by honest agreement on earth, peace and good will toward men is worthy of the greatest sacrifice a true man can bring. [71]

34

A Room of Quiet

The Meditation Room, a small, narrow trapezoid in the north corner of the public lobby at Headquarters Building, was designed by Hammarskjöld as a place where people of many faiths may meet with silence and feel "the void," the inexplicable connection between matter and spirit. The room is dim. A luminous mural by Bo Beskow seems to open a window to infinity, and a polished block of iron shimmers beneath a narrow shaft of light. There a visitor may sit and reflect upon the curious fancy of a Secretary-General who insisted that a house of argumentation should possess this room of quiet.

Outside the Meditation Room proper is an anteroom, the south wall of which is covered with magnificently patterned green Vermont marble, and on it are bronze plaques dedicated to the memory of those who have died in the service of the United Nations. Dag Hammarskjöld is among them, as are the fifteen colleagues who died with him, Count Bernadotte, who was assassinated in Palestine, and the many soldiers of the peace force still in the Congo and, until June of 1967, in the Gaza Strip.

Opposite, on the rosewood-paneled north wall is an abstract model of a ship, somewhat reminiscent of those legendary spectral ships that carried the souls of seafaring folk across measureless oceans.

The room was built with gifts from the Laymen's Movement,

which for the purpose of collecting funds organized a subgroup, consisting of Mohammedans, Jews, and Christians both Catholic and Protestant. On a little table in the anteroom is a visitors' book and next to it are leaflets to be taken home. The leaflets were written by Hammarskjöld, and those who read them in his lifetime could not have been too surprised when the publication of his diary, Markings, *revealed the Secretary-General to have lived in private the contemplating life of a mystic.*

Hammarskjöld was a frequent visitor to the room of quiet, and he visited it before he left on the journey to Africa from which he did not return. One of his last executive acts was to order a small marble plaque for the west wall of the anteroom. On it, engraved in black on black, hardly more conspicuous than a breath, one reads, "This is a room devoted to peace and those who are giving their lives for peace. It is a room of quiet where only thoughts should speak."

A   ROOM   OF   QUIET

The United Nations Meditation Room

> *This is a room devoted to peace*
> *and those who are giving their*
> *lives for peace. It is a room of quiet*
> *where only thoughts should speak.*

We all have within us a center of stillness surrounded by silence.

This house, dedicated to work and debate in the service of peace, should have one room dedicated to silence in the outward sense and stillness in the inner sense.

It has been the aim to create in this small room a place where the doors may be open to the infinite lands of thought and prayer.

People of many faiths will meet here, and for that reason none of the symbols to which we are accustomed in our meditation could be used.

However, there are simple things which speak to us all with the same language. We have sought for such things and we believe that we have found them in the shaft of light striking the shimmering surface of solid rock.

So, in the middle of the room we see a symbol of how, daily, the light of the skies gives life to the earth on which we stand, a symbol to many of us of how the light of the spirit gives life to matter.

But the stone in the middle of the room has more to tell us. We may see it as an altar, empty not because there is no God, not because it is an altar to an unknown god, but because it is dedicated to the God whom man worships under many names and in many forms.

The stone in the middle of the room reminds us also of the firm and permanent in a world of movement and change. The block of iron ore has the weight and solidity of the everlasting. It is a reminder of that cornerstone of endurance and faith on which all human endeavor must be based.

The material of the stone leads our thoughts to the necessity for choice between destruction and construction, between war and peace. Of iron man has forged his swords, of iron he has also made his ploughshares. Of iron he has constructed tanks, but of iron he has likewise built homes for man. The block of iron ore is part of the wealth we have inherited on this earth of ours. How are we to use it?

The shaft of light strikes the stone in a room of utter simplicity. There are no other symbols, there is nothing to distract our attention or to break in on the stillness within ourselves. When our eyes travel from these symbols to the front wall, they meet a simple pattern opening up the room to the harmony, freedom, and balance of space.

There is an ancient saying that the sense of a vessel is not in its shell but in the void. So it is with this room. It is for those who come here to fill the void with what they find in their center of stillness.

DAG HAMMARSKJÖLD
Secretary-General

35

International Conscience

Speaking before the American Association for the United Nations in 1953, Hammarskjöld said, "As individuals we can put our influence on the side of what we believe is right and true. We can help in the movement toward those ends that inspire our lives."

All of us, he believed, influence to some degree the spiritual trend of our time. All of us therefore may make our contribution to the compelling tasks that face us: breaking down the wall of distrust which stands between nations, and bringing to an end the fatal stalemate of conformism and sterile propaganda.

All we need is the courage to give voice to honest criticism when we see that something is wrong. We need "maturity of mind" reflected in the absence of fear, and recognition of the fact that fate is what we make it. It implies both pride and humility. We are satisfied to be what we are, but we refuse to seem more than we are; and we "give to our fellow men neither more nor less than what is really ours."

At the University of Lund in 1959 he said, "The health and strength of a community depend on every citizen's feeling of solidarity with the other citizens and on his willingness, in the name of this solidarity, to shoulder his part of the burdens of humanity as a whole."

⟨ The conflict between different approaches to the liberty of man and mind or between different views of human dignity and the right of the individual is continuous. The dividing line goes within ourselves, within our own peoples, and also within other nations. It does not coincide with any political or geographical boundaries. The ultimate fight is one between the human and the sub-human. We are on dangerous ground if we believe that any individual, any nation, or any ideology has a monoply on rightness, liberty, and human dignity. [11]

⟨ And just as it cannot be argued that within a community an economic upper class holds its favored position by virtue of greater ability, as a quality which is, as it were, vested in the group by nature, so it is, of course, impossible to maintain this in regard to nations in their mutual relationships. [80]

⟨ But let us not forget that there is a colonialism of the heart and of the mind, which no political decision can overcome and against which the battle must be waged within ourselves, without any exception. [73]

⟨ Our relations to our fellow men do not determine our attitude to ideals, but are determined by our ideals. If our attitude is consistent, we shall be consistent in our loyalties. If our attitude is confused, then our loyalties will also be divided. [26]

⟨ The United Nations has to activate in its support people's urge to live together and work together in peace and decency. For that reason the United Nations has to try to create a new awareness of human and national interdependence. In order to be able to do so it will have to understand what makes so difficult the development of such an awareness. It will have to understand—and challenge—the fear that motivates so much of human action, the fear that is our worst enemy but which, somehow, seems to taint at least some corner of the heart of every man. [22]

◖ It is easy to turn the responsibility over to others or, perhaps, to seek explanations in some kind of laws of history. It is less easy to look for the reasons within ourselves or in a field where we, all of us, carry a major responsibility. However, such a search is necessary, because finally it is only within ourselves and in such fields that we can hope, by our own actions, to make a valid contribution to a turn of the trend of events. [11]

◖ Each and every one of us is enabled to develop his own knowledge and judgment concerning the way that a society is growing and the way its leaders are trying to frame its future. [12]

◖ A mature man is his own judge. In the end, his only form of support is being faithful to his own convictions. The advice of others may be welcome and valuable, but it does not free him from responsibility. [81]

◖ Peace cannot be enforced for selfish reasons, equality cannot be imposed as an abstract concept. In fact, attempts to do so account for some of the darkest episodes in history. [34]

◖ All of us, in whatever field of intellectual activity we work, influence to some degree the spiritual trend of our time. All of us may contribute to the breakdown of the walls of distrust and toward checking fatal tendencies in the direction of stale conformism and propaganda. How can this be done better or more effectively than by simple faithfulness to the independence of the spirit and to the right of the free man to free thinking and free expression of his thoughts? [11]

◖ There is no formula to teach us how to arrive at maturity and there is no grammar for the language of inner life. His study, like the effort of every single individual, finally led him to the doorstep where the rest is silence because the rest is something that has to be resolved between a man and himself.

The results of the inner dialogue are evident to all, evident as independence, courage, and fairness in dealing with others, evident in true international service.

True, our duties to our families, our neighbors, our countries, our creeds have not changed. But something has been added. This is a duty to what I shall call international service, with a claim on our lives equal to that of the duty to serve within those smaller units whose walls are now breaking down. The international service of which I speak is not the special obligation, nor the privilege, of those working in international economic corporations, in the field of diplomacy, or in international political organizations. It has become today the obligation, as well as the privilege, of all.

We hear much about freedom and the blessings of freedom. We hear less about the obligations of freedom and the ideals by which freedom must be guided.

An individualism carried to the extreme where you neither accept restraint imposed on you by society, or by your fellow men, nor submit yourself to the laws of a mature conscience, would lead to anarchy. This is true no less of international life than of life within your own country. [26]

⟨ It is not the weak but the strong who practice tolerance, and the strong do not weaken their position in showing tolerance. [34]

⟨ No state, no group of states, no world organization, can grip the world and shape it, neither by force, nor by any formula of words in a charter or a treaty. There are no absolute answers to the agonies and searchings of our time. But all men and women of good will can influence the course of history in the direction of the ideals expressed in the Charter. [23]

⟨ The ultimate challenge to the political sciences—and to us all— is whether man shall master his world and his history or let himself be mastered by a world and a history which after all is made by man. There cannot be more than one reply to this question. Man must master his world, but in order to do so, he must know it. [22]

⟨ The dignity of man, as a justification for our faith in freedom, can be part of our living creed only if we revert to a view of life where maturity of mind counts for more than outward success and where happiness is no longer to be measured in quantitative terms. [26]

⟨ I suppose that, just as the first temptation of the realist is the illusion of cynicism, so the first temptation of the idealist is the illusion of Utopia. [31]

36

Peace Force

The United Nations was originally conceived—with optimism—on the principle of great-power unanimity. It was supposed that in times of crisis the great powers would collaborate to provide a peace force to restore order. In case this happy event should ever come to pass, the Charter provided for a Military Staff Committee composed of military men representing the great powers. It exists to this day.

As it happened, great-power unanimity did not even survive the San Francisco Conference which brought the United Nations to birth, and the unseating of Mainland China placed one mighty power outside the Organization entirely. Thus we have once more, as we had in the League of Nations, a World Organization without effective means of enforcing its decisions. However, during Hammarskjöld tenure of office, such grave need arose for a peace-keeping force that the Secretary-General was obliged to organize it over the heads of the paralyzed Military Staff Committee.

On October 29, 1956, Israel invaded the Sinai Peninsula. Within two days British and French bombers had attacked Egyptian airfields, and motorized units were well on their way to Cairo. An emergency Assembly met in New York which called upon the Secretary-General to undertake the necessary steps to "secure and supervise the cessation of hostilities." The step Hammarskjöld took was a spectacular one: With amazing speed he brought into being an international peace-keeping force known as the UNEF—the United Nations Emergency Force. By November 12 the first UNEF troops had landed on Egyptian soil, separating the belligerents.

Two years later, Hammarskjöld prepared a summary and analysis of this experience, telling how the force was organized at short notice and how such a force could be expected to operate in any emergency. He had intended to present it to the General Assembly "to afford useful guidance for any future effort" in which armed force might be called for. Though this item was on the agenda of the thirteenth Session of the General Assembly in 1958, the document never reached the Assembly floor. The Soviet Union warned Hammarskjöld in the Special Political Committee that if he submitted his summary analysis they would tear it apart.

Four years after Hammarskjöld's death a Special Committee on Peacekeeping (Committee 33) was formed to discuss the question of a possible peace force, and it is still in session. Because the Secretary-General is still a controversial figure, the committee holds aloof, at least publicly, from his summary analysis, but in dark privacy one presumes, and hopes, they study it. Officially the study lies deeply buried in the archives of the United Nations under a tombstone marked Document A/3943. Following are some excerpts from this little-known document.

⟪ UNEF represents a new and in many ways unique experiment by the United Nations in a type of operation which previously it had not been called upon to conduct.

The force was created as a temporary measure, its characteristics were determined by the nature of its role, and its functions were defined and limited by decisions of the General Assembly applying to a particular set of circumstances.

This report presents a summary analysis of the organization and operation of the force. . . . The emphasis is on those principles and conclusions which emerge from a study of the operation as a whole and which might afford useful guidance for any future efforts looking toward the establishment or use of international United Nations instruments serving purposes of the kind met by UNEF.

The first resolution adopted by the General Assembly when it began consideration of the military operations against Egyptian territory (resolution 997 (ES-I) of 2 November 1956) was directed primarily and as a matter of priority toward obtaining an immediate cessation of hostilities, a halting of the movement of military forces and arms into the area, a full observance of the provisions of the armistice agreements, and the reopening of the Suez Canal.

The question of setting up an emergency international United Nations force followed closely upon the adoption of that resolution. It grew out of the increasing recognition by Members that extraordinary measures had to be taken in order to achieve all the objectives sought by the resolution.

The General Assembly, in its resolution 1000 (ES-I) of 5 November 1956, provided that the force would "secure and supervise the cessation of hostilities in accordance with all the terms" of resolution 997 (ES-I) of 2 November, which would include the withdrawal of non-Egyptian forces from Egyptian territory and the restoration of observance of the provisions of the General Armistice Agreement between Egypt and Israel.

This new instrument was charged with a dual role: initially to secure and supervise the cease-fire and the withdrawal of armed forces from Egyptian territory, and later to maintain peaceful conditions in the area by its deployment along the Egyptian-Israel armistice demarcation line in the Gaza area and to the south along the international frontier.

There was "no intent . . . to influence the military balance in the present conflict and, thereby, the political balance affecting efforts to settle the conflict." Nor was the force to be "used so as to prejudge the solution of the controversial questions involved."

It was felt, moreover, that the creation of peaceful conditions in the area required avoidance of the state of affairs into which conditions had progressively deteriorated in the past as a result of the lack of full implementation of the clauses of the Armistice Agreement. The objective sought was to ensure strict compliance by Egypt and Israel with the letter and spirit of the General Armistice Agreement concluded between them.

The deployment of the force along the Israel-Egyptian armistice demarcation line and the international frontier south of Gaza, and in the Sharm el Sheikh area, was not meant to and could not effect any change in their prior *status juris;* its sole purpose was to maintain quiet and prevent the recurrence of incidents.

The concept of a force established on this basis is basically different from that by which the United Nations might entrust a country, or a group of countries, with the responsibility of providing independently for an international force serving purposes determined by the Organization, as in the case of the Unified Command in Korea. It is also different from the concept, for which there is no precedent in application, of an international force set up by agreement among a group of nations, later to be brought into some appropriate relationship with the United Nations.

The functions of the force are exclusively international in character in that they relate to armed conflict among States.

UNEF has been necessarily limited in its operations to the

extent that consent of the parties concerned is required under generally recognized international law. It followed that, while the General Assembly could establish the force, subject only to the concurrence of the States providing contingents, the consent of the Government of the country concerned was required before the Assembly could request the force to be stationed or to operate on the territory of that country. The force has no rights other than those necessary for the execution of the functions assigned to it by the General Assembly and agreed to by the country or countries concerned.

The force is paramilitary in character and much more than an observer corps, but it is in no sense a military force exercising, through force of arms, even temporary control over the territory in which it is stationed; nor does it have military objectives, or military functions exceeding those necessary to secure peaceful conditions on the assumption that the parties to the conflict will take all the necessary steps for compliance with the recommendations of the General Assembly.

The force is composed of national contingents accepted for service by the Secretary-General from among those voluntarily offered by Member States.

In the case of UNEF, the policy has been to exclude military personnel belonging to any of the permanent members of the Security Council and from any country which for geographical or other reasons might have a special interest in the conflict.

The choice of the contingents for the force, while subject to the decision of the United Nations alone, is nevertheless of major concern also to the country in which the force operates. Thus, the United Nations must give most serious consideration to the views of the host government on such matters without, however, surrendering its right to take a serious difference, should one develop, to the political level for resolution.

The size of component units has been determined by two primary requirements. From the point of view of efficiency, it was necessary that Member States should provide units sufficiently large to be relatively self-contained. From the point of view of balance, it was desirable that the force should include adequate support elements and that the differences in the size of units should not be so great as to lead to excessive dependence on any one State.

In practice, the UNEF operation is an example of fruitful military and civilian collaboration. Matters relating to its administration and finance, communications, maintenance, and other services are taken care of within the framework of the United Nations Secretariat.

The regulations for the force affirm its international character as a subsidiary organ of the General Assembly. The Assembly intended that the force should be a temporary arrangement, whose duration would be determined by the needs created by the emergency, and whose tasks and legal basis could be defined only by the Assembly.

In conjunction with the establishment of the force, the General Assembly decided to create an Advisory Committee composed of seven representatives of Member States, under the chairmanship of the Secretary-General. In its advisory capacity, this committee was to assist the Secretary-General in the planning and operation of the force. It was empowered to request, through the usual procedures, the convening of the General Assembly and to report to the Assembly, if matters should arise which, in its opinion, were of such urgency and importance as to require consideration by the Assembly itself.

There was urgent need to assemble a usable force, as rapidly as possible, and to land it in Egypt. While awaiting the conclusion of arrangements with Egypt for the entry of the force into that country, it was decided that a staging area near the Mediterranean would be necessary, as it would expedite the flow of troops and *matériel* to Egypt. Arrangements were quickly made with the Government of Italy for the use of Capodichino Airport, Naples, for this purpose. Most of the troops brought to Egypt by air were sent via Naples, others were flown in via Beirut, while others came by sea to Port Said. The small staff in charge of the staging area at Capodichino took care of the incoming (and later outgoing) contingents, dealt with the several authorities in Europe through whom major logistic support was obtained, supervised the airlift to Egypt and arranged for the surface transport of heavy stores.

The initial movements of troops from their home bases to Italy were arranged through United Nations Headquarters. The problems were mainly transportation and coordination. The bulk of the transport to the staging area was provided by the United States Air Force.

Advance elements of UNEF were moved to Egypt at a time when hostilities had but recently ceased; there were restrictions on the times and lanes of flights, and aircraft transporting contingents had to be of suitable nationalities. The initial airlift of troops to Abu Suweir was carried out by Swissair. The Naples to Egypt airlift was subsequently taken over by the Royal Canadian Air Force with some assistance from the Italian Air Force in lifting supplies.

All heavy equipment for UNEF was brought in by ship.

The clear identification of UNEF personnel, beyond the customary United Nations armbands, was an immediate necessity for security and other reasons. Light blue helmet liners with United Nations markings were adopted for this purpose, and were later supplemented by blue berets and desert caps and UNEF badges and insignia. Vehicles and aircraft were painted white with United Nations markings.

In the period November–December 1956, twenty-four Member States offered to provide units. A number of these countries also offered other forms of assistance, as did two other Member States and one nonmember. Most of the offers of assistance were of infantry units. The force, at the peak of its strength totaling about 6,000 officers and men, consisted of contingents from the following countries: Brazil, Canada, Colombia, Denmark, Finland, India, Indonesia, Norway, Sweden, and Yugoslavia.

The original plan of operations assumed that in compliance with General Assembly resolutions, Israeli troops would, after the cease-fire, withdraw within a short time behind the armistice demarcation line and that the force would then be deployed along the Egyptian-Israeli armistice demarcation line and the international frontier south of the Gaza Strip.

On the whole, the functions performed by the force in the Sinai Peninsula were similar to those undertaken in the Suez Canal area. It was interposed between the forces of Egypt and Israel from 3 December 1956 onward; it undertook temporarily some local civic responsibilities, including security functions, in a few inhabited areas during the successive stages of the withdrawal of Israel, handing over all such responsibilities to the Egyptian authorities as soon as they returned to their posts; it arranged and carried out the exchange of prisoners of war between Egypt and Israel; it discharged certain investigatory functions; it cleared minefields in the Sinai Peninsula; and it repaired temporarily portions of damaged roads and tracks crossing the Peninsula, necessary for the conduct of its operations.

UNEF troops have a right to fire in self-defense. They are

never to take the initiative in the use of arms, but may respond with fire to an armed attack upon them, even though this may result from a refusal on their part to obey an order from the attacking party not to resist; a proper refusal, since they are to take orders only from the commander. UNEF is authorized to apprehend infiltrators and persons approaching the demarcation line in suspicious circumstances.

The functioning of UNEF in the field is the direct responsibility of the commander, who serves both as the director of operations and as the supervisor of all other activities of the force.

The commander holds office through appointment by the General Assembly. He operates under the instructions and guidance of the Secretary-General on the basis of executive responsibility for the operation entrusted to him by the Assembly. In practice, from the inception of the force, the commander has functioned as the principal agent of the Secretary-General in the area of operations, within the limits of his post.

The contingents receive their instructions and direction from the commander, advised and assisted by his staff. The commanding officers of the units are held responsible by the commander for the proper functioning and discipline of their personnel. The contingent commanders are free to communicate with their home Governments on all matters affecting their units.

Some of the contributing governments designated "liaison officers" to represent their interests on the scene of operations of UNEF and to serve as points of contact for them. These liaison officers, not being under the authority of the commander, are not members of UNEF. Their status, therefore, is rather anomalous. In practice, the liaison officer's function has worked best when the officer concerned was one assigned to a UNEF post having important duties in its own right.

Administratively, responsibility for UNEF rests with the Secretary-General, in order to ensure that the operation will be executed in a manner consistent with the established practices and administrative principles of the United Nations. The day-to-day responsibilities of administration are exercised by the commander of the force, assisted by the senior Secretariat officials assigned by the Secretary-General to the force.

From the very beginning of the operation, the Secretariat has assigned public information officers to UNEF. They report directly to the commander. Their principal function has been to assist in press relations with correspondents assigned to cover the force.

UNEF's own weekly newspaper, *Sand Dune,* is edited and published under their guidance.

A United Nations Welfare Officer was appointed to supervise all welfare activities including the provision of reading material, films, PX facilities, sports equipment, and, when possible, live entertainment. Inter-contingent sporting events are an important feature of the recreation program. Units also organize their own entertainment from the very considerable talent available in their various national ranks. Leave centers were established in Beirut on 1 May 1957, in Cairo in November 1957 for the winter months, and again in Beirut and later Alexandria in 1958. Occasional tours to historic places have also been arranged.

The relations of UNEF with the local population have in general been good and no serious incidents have occurred, except for one on 10 March 1957. The Gaza Strip, with its large refugee population, is a sensitive area where particularly strict standards of behavior and respect for local customs have been necessary and have been adhered to by members of the force. The order issued in November 1957 that troops should carry arms only when on duty has been a factor in good relations. Along the international frontier, with its sparse and largely nomadic population, a tradition of goodwill and cooperation has also been built up, to the advantage of both parties. At the leave centers—whether in Beirut, Cairo, or Alexandria—relations with the local populations have posed no serious problems.

In considering general stand-by arrangements for United Nation operations of the kind envisaged in this report, a course should be followed which would afford a considerable degree of flexibility in approaching the varying needs that may arise.

The type and rank of military personnel required, the need for specialists and for supporting units, as well as the vehicle and equipment demands, as experience has shown, also vary so much from case to case that more far-reaching and firm arrangements—as, for example, the maintenance of a nucleus United Nations force of the type generally envisaged—would be without great practical value and certainly would not warrant the substantial sacrifices involved.

To meet adequately the requirements of a given situation, a broad decision by the General Assembly should attempt to do no more than endorse certain basic principles and rules which would provide an adaptable framework for later operations that might be found necessary. In a practical sense, it is not feasible in advance of a known situation to do more than to provide for some helpful stand-by arrangements for a force or similar forms of a United Nations presence.

It follows from international law and the Charter that the United Nations cannot undertake stationing units on the territory of a Member State without the consent of the government concerned. It similarly follows from the Charter that the consent of a Member nation is necessary for the United Nations to use its military personnel or *matériel*. These basic rules have been observed in the recent United Nations operations in the Middle

East. They naturally hold valid for all similar operations in the future.

[*The following four items were supplemented by Hammarskjöld by a private understanding with Nasser which became the subject of the much-debated memorandum discussed in the next chapter.*]

The fact that a United Nations operation of the type envisaged requires the consent of the government on whose territory it takes place creates a problem, as it is normally difficult for the United Nations to engage in such an operation without guarantees against unilateral actions by the host government which might put the United Nations in a questionable position, either administratively or in relation to contributing governments.

The formula employed in relation to the government of Egypt for UNEF seems, in the light of experience, to provide an adequate solution to this problem. The government of Egypt declared that, when exercising its sovereign right with regard to the presence of the force, it would be guided by good faith in the interpretation of the purposes of the force. This declaration was balanced by a declaration by the United Nations to the effect that the maintenance of the force by the United Nations would be determined by similar good faith in the interpretation of the purposes.

The consequence of such a bilateral declaration is that, were either side to act unilaterally in refusing continued presence or deciding on withdrawal, and were the other side to find that such action was contrary to a good-faith interpretation of the purposes of the operation, an exchange of views would be called for toward harmonizing the positions. This does not imply any infringement of the sovereign right of the host government, nor any restriction of the right of the United Nations to decide on the termination of its own operation whenever it might see fit to do so. But it does mean a mutual recognition of the fact that the operation, being based on collaboration between the host government and the United Nations, should be carried on in forms natural to such collaboration, and especially so with regard to the questions of presence and maintenance.

It is unlikely that any government in the future would be willing to go beyond the declaration of the Government of Egypt with regard to UNEF. Nor, in my view, should the United Nations commit itself beyond the point established for UNEF in relation to the Government of Egypt. In these circumstances, I consider it reasonable to regard the formula mentioned above as a valid basis for future arrangements of a similar kind.

Another point of principle which arises in relation to the question of consent refers to the composition of United Nations military elements stationed on the territory of a Member country. While the United Nations must reserve for itself the authority to decide on the composition of such elements, it is obvious that the host country, in giving its consent, cannot be indifferent to the composition of those elements. In order to limit the scope of possible difference of opinion, the United Nations in recent operations has followed two principles: not to include units from any of the permanent members of the Security Council; and not to include units from any country which, because of its geographical position or for other reasons, might be considered as possibly having a special interest in the situation which has called for the operation. I believe that these two principles also should be considered as essential to any stand-by arrangements.

I would recommend that the basis thus laid in the case of UNEF be considered as the formula on composition applicable to similar operations in the future.

The most important principle in the status agreement ensures that UNEF personnel, when involved in criminal actions, come under the jurisdiction of the criminal courts of their home countries. . . . Experience shows that this principle is essential to the successful recruitment by the United Nations of military personnel not otherwise under immunity rules, from its Member countries. The position established for UNEF should be maintained in future arrangements.

Authority granted to the United Nations group cannot be exercised within a given territory either in competition with representatives of the host government or in cooperation with them on the basis of any joint operation. Thus, a United Nations operation must be separate and distinct from activities by national authorities.

United Nations personnel cannot be permitted in any sense to be a party to internal conflicts. Their role must be limited to external aspects of the political situation as, for example, infiltration or other activities affecting international boundaries.

In setting up UNEF, the General Assembly appointed a commander of the force with the position of an international civil servant responsible for the discharge of his task to the Assembly, but administratively integrated with the United Nations Organization, and under instructions from the Secretary-General on the basis of the executive authority for the operation vested in him by the Assembly.

A United Nations operation should always be under a leadership established by the General Assembly or the Security Council, or on the basis of delegated authority by the Secretary-General, so as to make it directly responsible to one of the main organs of the United Nations, while integrated with the Secretariat in an appropriate form.

A formal decision on a United Nations operation must be taken by the General Assembly or by the Security Council. It must be regarded as excluded that the right to take such a decision, in any general terms, could properly be considered as delegated to the Secretary-General. Short of an explicit decision by the General Assembly or the Security Council with a specific authorization, the Secretary-General, thus, cannot be considered as entitled to appeal to a Member nation for military personnel to be dispatched to another Member country in a United Nations operation.

The terms of the delegation in each operation thus far have set the limit of the Secretary-General's authority. Thus, for example, as is apparent from the description of the new body, the decision relating to the UNEF, which was to be implemented by the Secretary-General, qualified the operation as being one of a paramilitary nature, while the absence of an explicit authorization for the force to take offensive action excluded the organization by the Secretary-General of units for such action, and consequently, the units generally were equipped only with weapons necessary for self-defense. Had there been any remaining doubts in this respect, the legal basis on which the General Assembly took its decision would have made this limitation clear.

A Member country, in deciding upon a contribution of men or *matériel* to a United Nations operation on the basis of such stand-by understandings as may have been reached, could rely upon the explicit terms of the executive authority delegated to the Secretary-General in determining the use which could be made of the units provided; it being understood, naturally, that in the types of operation with which this report is concerned this could never include combat activity. There will always remain, of course, a certain margin of freedom for judgment, as, for example, on the extent and nature of the arming of the units and of their right of self-defense. In the case of UNEF, such questions of interpretation have been solved in consultation with the contributing governments and with the host government.

I have touched upon the extent to which a right of self-defense may be exercised by United Nations units of the type envisaged. It should be generally recognized that such a right exists. However, in certain cases this right should be exercised only under strictly defined conditions. A problem arises in this context because of the fact that a wide interpretation of the right of self-defense might well blur the distinction between operations of the character discussed in this report and combat operations, which would require a decision under Chapter VII of the Charter and an explicit, more far-reaching delegation of authority to the Secretary-General than would be required for any of the operations discussed here.

Men engaged in the operation may never take the initiative in the use of armed force, but are entitled to respond with force to an attack with arms, including attempts to use force to make them withdraw from positions which they occupy under orders from the commander, acting under the authority of the Assembly and within the scope of its resolutions. The element involved is clearly the prohibition against any *initiative* in the use of armed force. This definition of the limit between self-defense, as permissible for United Nations elements of the kind discussed, and offensive action, which is beyond the competence of such elements, should be approved for future guidance.

In the case of UNEF, the General Assembly decided to organize an Advisory Committee, under the chairmanship of the Secretary-General, to assist the operation. In practice, this arrangement has proved highly useful. In principle, it should be accepted as a precedent for the future.

The Advisory Committee is fully informed by the Secretary-General and his associates. There is a free exchange of views in closed meetings where advice can be sought and given. But ultimate decisions rest with the Secretary-General, as the executive in charge of carrying out the operation. Dissenting views are not registered by vote, but are put on record in the proceedings of the committee. It is useful for contributing countries to be represented on such an advisory committee, but if the contributing States are numerous the size of the committee might become so large as to make it ineffective.

The question, however, is of interest in this context, as it has a bearing on the problem whether or not such stand-by arrangements as those for which the principles and rules set out here would provide, would call for any kind of nucleus of military experts at United Nations Headquarters. At some stage, a standing group of a few military experts might be useful in order to keep under review such arrangements as may be made by governments of Member States in preparation for meeting possible appeals for an operation. I would consider it premature, however, to take any decision of this kind at the present time, since the foreseeable tasks that might evolve for the Secretariat do not go beyond what it is now able to cope with unassisted by such special measures. Were a more far-reaching understanding than I have indicated to prove possible, the matter obviously would have to be reconsidered and submitted again in appropriate form to the General Assembly, which then might consider the organizational problem. Pending such a development later, the present working rule, in my view, should be that the Secretariat, while undertaking the soundings mentioned above and the necessary continuing contacts with the governments, should not take any measures beyond keeping the situation under constant review, so as to be able to act expeditiously, if a decision by the General Assembly or the Security Council should call for prompt action.

It may be reiterated in passing that the United Nations Secretariat has by now had extensive experience in establishing and maintaining United Nations operations involving military personnel and, without improvising or augmenting unduly, can quickly provide any operation of that nature with efficient communications service in the field and with Headquarters, with transportation and vehicles for local transport, with well-tested administrative and accounting systems and expert personnel to man them, and with effective procurement and security arrangements.

The financial obligations of Member countries to the United Nations are of two kinds. On the one hand, there are such obligations as are covered by the scale of contributions established by the General Assembly; on the other, there are certain voluntary commitments outside that scale, such as United Nations technical assistance or the United Nations Children's Fund.

With relation to the men engaged in one of its operations, the United Nations should naturally assume all responsibilities necessary to safeguard the normal interest of those so employed. Thus, they should be fully compensated by the United Nations for any losses of earning power or social benefits which may be suffered because of their service with the United Nations.

With relation to a host government, it should be the rule that as the United Nations units are dispatched to the country in the interest and with the consent and cooperation of the host government, that government should provide all necessary facilities for the operation. This, in principle, should be done without any compensation, in cases where such facilities are in the possession of the host government itself. Thus, for example, contributions of government services or government-owned property placed at the disposal of the United Nations for its operation should not be subject to compensation.

Concerning the claims of private citizens in the host country, the applicable rule is that the United Nations should pay compensation for the use of their property or services, whenever the host government would have been obligated to pay for similar services or uses. The question whether the United Nations, in its turn, should be reimbursed by the host government for such outlays would properly be settled through negotiation, in the light of the circumstances in each separate case.

The United Nations, within the limits of the Charter, may seek the most practical method of mustering and using, as necessary, the resources—both of nations and its own—required for operations involving military personnel which may be conceived in response to the needs of specific conflict situations.

The national resources likely to be available for such purposes, if our limited experience is a gauge, are no doubt substantial, but they cannot now be calculated or even estimated, and even their availability at any particular time would probably be subject to considerable fluctuation, for political and other reasons. Formalizing the principles and rules outlined above, however, would afford a strengthened basis on which to expedite the mobilization of voluntary aid toward meeting urgent need. Their approval by the Assembly, thus clarifying and regularizing important legal and practical issues, would also ensure a more efficient use of any aid extended to the Organization, were it again to have to appeal to Member nations for such assistance.

37

The Hammarskjöld Memorandum

On May 18, 1967, President Gamal Abdel Nasser of the United Arab Republic requested the withdrawal of the United Nations Emergency Force from the Israeli-Egyptian armistice demarcation line. Secretary-General U Thant promptly complied and, as we know, on June 5, 1967, hostilities broke out again in the Middle East. President Johnson and other Western leaders criticized U Thant for his "hurried" action, and Foreign Minister Abba Eban of Israel called the withdrawal decision "disastrously swift."

On June 18, 1967, Ambassador Ernest A. Gross, a former United States deputy representative at the United Nations and a consultant to Hammarskjöld, revealed the contents of a memorandum given to him by the late Secretary-General. It had been written on August 5, 1957, nine months after the establishment of the peace force. Hammarskjöld had told friends that he was dissatisfied with the public and legal discussions of the arrangements, which he felt were vague and ambiguous, and he had felt obliged, therefore, to deposit in United Nations files some of the history of his negotiations in Cairo; and he insisted that all interpretations of the agreement "must" be governed by this memorandum.

The memorandum described a private seven-hour conversation between Hammarskjöld and Nasser, which had taken place in Cairo on November 17, 1956. The two men arranged that the United Nations would not withdraw its forces, and that Cairo *would not order them withdrawn, until both agreed that the troops had completed their task. This task was defined by the United Nations Assembly resolution "to secure and supervise the cessation of hostilities."*

Hammarskjöld wrote that under the formula he had devised, any Egyptian request for withdrawal of the forces had to be brought before the General Assembly at once. It was up to the Assembly to decide whether the force had completed its task or not.

According to the memorandum, the Egyptian government had reluctantly adhered to Hammarskjöld's formula because Nasser at that time was eager to have the peace force stationed on Egyptian territory in order to force a withdrawal of Israeli troops from the territory they had seized in the Sinai Peninsula.

Excerpts from the Hammarskjöld memorandum follow.

❪ As the decision of the UNEF (United Nations Emergency Force) was taken under Chapter VI (of the Charter) it was obvious from the beginning that the resolution did in no way limit the sovereignty of the host state.

Neither the General Assembly nor the Secretary-General, acting for the General Assembly, created any right for Egypt, or gave any right to Egypt, in accepting consent as a condition for the presence and functioning of the UNEF on Egyptian territory. Egypt had the right, and the only problem was whether that right in this context should and could in some way be limited.

My starting point in the consideration of this last-mentioned problem—the limitation of Egypt's sovereign right in the interest of political balance and stability in the UNEF operation—was the fact that Egypt had spontaneously endorsed the General Assembly resolution of 5 November (creating the force) and by endorsing that resolution had consented to the presence of the UNEF for certain tasks. They could thus not ask the UNEF to withdraw before the completion of the tasks without running up against their own acceptance of the resolution on the force and its tasks.

Egypt had requested clarification of the question how long it was contemplating that the force would stay in the demarcation line area. To this I replied the same day: "A definite reply is at present impossible, but the emergency character of the force links it to the immediate crisis envisaged in the resolution of 2 November (calling for truce) and its liquidation. In case of different views as to when the crisis does not any longer warrant the presence of the troops, the matter will have to be negotiated with the parties.

"I want to put on record that the conditions which motivate the consent to entry and presence are the very conditions to which the tasks established for the force in the General Assembly resolution (requesting preparations for establishment of the force), 4 November, are directed. Therefore I assume it to be recognized that as long as the task, thus prescribed, is not completed, the reasons for the consent of the government remain valid, and that a withdrawal of this consent before completion of the task would run counter to the acceptance by Egypt of the decision of the General Assembly. I read the statement quoted in the light of these considerations. If a difference should develop, whether or not the reasons for the arrangements are still valid, the matter should be brought up for negotiation with the United Nations."

This explanation of mine was sent to the Egyptian mission after my telephone conversation in the morning of the 12th with Dr. Fawzi where we agreed on publication of our agreement on the entry of the UNEF into Egypt. In view of the previous exchanges, I had no reason to believe that my statement would introduce any new difficulty.

However, I recognized to myself that there was an element of gambling involved which I felt I simply had to take in view of the danger that further delays might cause Egypt to change its mind, accept volunteers, and throw our approaches overboard.

I had a feeling that it now was a must to get the troops in and that I would be in a position to find a formula, saving the face of Egypt while protecting the United Nations stand, once I would discuss the matter personally with President Nasser.

I said that my previous statements had put forward my personal opinion that "the reasons" for consent remained valid as long as the task was not completed. I also said that for that reason a withdrawal of consent leading to the withdrawal of the force before the task was completed (as previously stated) in my view, "although within the rights of the Egyptian Government would go against its acceptance of the basic resolution of the General Assembly."

I commented upon the official reply in a special personal message to Fawzi, sent at the same time, where I said that we "both had to reserve our freedom of action, but that, all the same, we could go ahead, hoping that a controversial situation would not arise." "If arrangements would break down on this issue" (withdrawal only on completion of the tasks), "I could not avoid going to the General Assembly" (with the conflict which had developed between us on this question of principle) "putting it to their judgment to decide what could or could not be accepted as an understanding. This situation would be a most embarrassing one for all but I would fear the political repercussions, as obviously very few would find it reasonable that recognition of your freedom of action should mean that you, after having permitted the force to come, might ask it to withdraw at a time when the very reasons which had previously prompted you to accept were still obviously valid."

I was guided by the consideration that Egypt constitutionally had an undisputed right to request the withdrawal of the troops, even if initial consent had been given, but that, on the other hand, it should be possible on the basis of my own stand as finally tacitly accepted, to force them into an agreement in which they limited their freedom of action as to withdrawal by making a request for withdrawal dependent upon the completion of the task—a question which, in the United Nations, obviously would have to be submitted to interpretation by the General Assembly.

The most desirable thing, of course, would have been to tie Egypt by an agreement in which they declared that withdrawal should take place only if so decided by the General Assembly. But in this naked form, however, the problem could never have been settled. I felt that the same was true of an agreement to the effect that withdrawal should take place upon "agreement on withdrawal" between the United Nations and the Egyptian Government. However, I found it worthwhile to try a line, very close to the second one, according to which Egypt would declare to the United Nations that it would exert all its sovereign rights with regard to the troops on the basis of a good faith interpretation of the tasks of the force. The United Nations should make a reciprocal commitment to maintain the force as long as the task was not completed.

If such a dual statement was introduced in an agreement between the parties, it would be obvious that the procedure in case of a request from Egypt for the withdrawal of UNEF would be as follows. The matter would at once be brought before the General Assembly. If the General Assembly found that the task was completed, everything would be all right. If they found that the task was not completed and Egypt, all the same, maintained its stand and enforced the withdrawal, Egypt would break the agreement with the United Nations.

Of course Egypt's freedom of action could under no circumstances be limited but by some kind of agreement. The device I used meant only that instead of limiting their rights by a basic understanding requesting an agreement *directly concerning withdrawal*, we created an obligation to reach agreement on the fact that the tasks were completed, and thus, *the conditions for a withdrawal established*.

I discussed practically only this issue with Nasser for seven hours in the evening and night of 17 November. Nasser, in this final discussion, where the text I had proposed was approved with some amendments, showed that he very fully understood that, by limiting their freedom of action in the way I proposed, they would take a very serious step, as it would mean that the question of the extent of the task would become decisive for the relations between Egypt and the United Nations and would determine Egypt's political freedom of action. He felt, not without justification, that the definition given of the task in the United Nations texts was very loose and that tying the freedom of action of Egypt to the concept of the task—which had to be interpreted also by the General Assembly—and doing so in a written agreement meant that he accepted a far-reaching and unpredictable restriction.

To push the text through, in spite of Nasser's determination to avoid this, and his strong suspicion of the legal construction—especially of the possible consequences of differences of views regarding the task—I felt obliged, in the course of the discussion, to threaten three times that, unless an agreement of this type was made, I would have to propose the immediate withdrawal of the troops. If any proof would be necessary for how the text of the agreement was judged by President Nasser, this last-mentioned fact tells the story.

The publication of the Hammarskjöld memorandum in The New York Times *on June 19, 1967, caused considerable controversy. In a report to the Fifth Emergency Special Assembly on June 26, Secretary-General U Thant defended his actions and replied: "It is understood that Mr. Hammarskjöld often prepared private notes concerning significant events under the heading 'aide-mémoire.' This memorandum is not in any official record of the United Nations nor is it in any of the official files. The General Assembly, the Advisory Committee on UNEF, and the Government of Egypt were not informed of its contents or existence. It is not an official paper and has no standing beyond being a purely private memorandum of unknown purpose or value, in which*

Secretary-General Hammarskjöld seems to record his own impressions and interpretations of his discussions with President Nasser. This paper, therefore, cannot affect in any way the basis for the presence of UNEF on the soil of the United Arab Republic as set out in the official documents, much less supersede those documents. . . ."

When the UNEF was set up, two resolutions defining its role were adopted by the General Assembly. One, on November 5, 1956, described its task in very general terms as being "to secure and supervise the cessation of hostilities." In U Thant's view, that task had been completed, since hostilities had ceased automatically once the UNEF was deployed; and the armistice had prevailed for eighteen years.

The second resolution had been adopted on February 2, 1957, and it broadened the function of the UNEF "to assure the scrupulous maintenance of the armistice agreements." This broader task, U Thant said, had not been completed, nor would it be possible to say at the present time when it would or could be completed. But he pointed out that the private understanding referred to in the November 17, 1956, memorandum between Hammarskjöld and Nasser could only refer to the task as defined in the November 5 resolution, which was completed. It could not refer to the broader task as defined on February 2, 1957, two and a half months later.

Egypt, U Thant pointed out, had always taken the public position that "the General Assembly could not request the UNEF to be stationed or to operate on the territory of a given country without the consent of the government of the country."

U Thant further noted that the Hammarskjöld memorandum did not touch upon a decisive point: the matter of stationing the UNEF on both sides of the armistice line. U Thant stated: "Israel, in the exercise of its sovereign right, did not give its consent to the stationing of the UNEF on its territory, and Egypt did not forego its sovereign right to withdraw its consent at any time."

As for the suggestion that the final decision on the withdrawal of the UNEF should have been taken only after consideration by the General Assembly, the Secretary-General said, "This position is not only incorrect, but also unrealistic. . . .

"As a practical matter, there would be little point in any case in taking such an issue to the General Assembly unless there would be reasonable certainty that that body could be expected expeditiously to reach a substantive decision. In the prevailing circumstances, the question could have been validly raised as to what decision other than the withdrawal of the UNEF could have been reached by the Assembly once United Arab Republic consent for the continued presence of the UNEF was withdrawn."

In rebuttal of the criticism that the withdrawal of the UNEF was a prime cause for the outbreak of war in the Near East, Secretary-General U Thant said, "This is, of course, a superficial and over-simplified approach. . . . This view ignores the fact that the underlying basis for this and other crisis situations in the Near East is the continuing Arab-Israel conflict which has been present all along and of which the crisis situation created by the unexpected withdrawal of UNEF is the latest expression."

A "background release," dated June 3, 1967, further stated that "it is merely confusing to . . . indulge in the sophistry that the conflict would have been solved simply if the UNEF had stayed on. This, manifestly, it could not have done."

A melancholy footnote to this dispute might be that until an international judiciary is set up, with a peace force as an executive arm, such a force can be effective only as long as the parties it separates do not wish to go to war.

38

The Perils of His Office

*In 1961 the Congo was in a state of crisis, and Hammarskjöld
was deeply in trouble. The Soviet Union labeled him a "sorry
lackey of the colonialists," and the Communist bloc refused to
recognize him as the Secretary-General of the United Nations.
Western countries with mining interests in the Congo, while
publicly supporting him, were equally dissatisfied with his
handling of the troubled situation, and in private let him know
about it.*

*In May 1961 he delivered a lecture before Congregation at
Oxford which, although it was mainly a general discussion of
International Civil Service, reflected his immediate anxieties.
Drawing upon bitter experience, he noted several perils of the
Secretary-General's office. A situation might arise, he said, when
the organs—the Security Council and the General Assembly—un-
able to resolve a controversial issue themselves, left it to the
Secretary-General to resolve "on his own risk." If his action ran
counter to the view of some Member States—as it unavoidably
must—he was exposed to the charge that he had abandoned the
political neutrality essential to his office.*

*Again, Member States, after voting for a decision and entrusting
its execution to the Secretary-General, might nevertheless base
their policies on reservations they had expressed in their explana-*

tion of vote. Almost any action of the Secretary-General must then be open to renewed controversy.

Quite often a State, having cast its vote in favor of a decision, later reinterprets the decision in ways that seem to differ from the wishes of the Council. It is particularly dangerous when one of the great powers backs away from a resolution in this manner.

There is also the situation when agreements reached and re-solved upon in fairly precise terms are rendered controversial by some unforeseen development. In the case of the Congo, a unanimous resolution was passed authorizing assistance to the Central Government; but when the government split into com-peting factions, each claiming to be the Central Government, and each supported by different groups of Member States within and outside the Security Council, the Secretary-General's implementa-tion of the decision could only arouse ire. "Implementation obvi-ously means interpretation," said Hammarskjöld wryly before the Council.

"I have the right to expect guidance," he said, "but if the Security Council says nothing, I have no other choice than to follow my convictions."

The convictions of a Secretary-General are not necessarily those of a party in conflict; they also permit him some "interpretations" of his own. Hammarskjöld saw Article 99 of the Charter as the fountainhead of the Secretary-General's political power. Since the article enjoins the Secretary-General to call to the attention of the Security Council matters which in his opinion *endanger peace and security, surely he must have the right to* form his opinion *by making a preliminary inquiry. And if, indeed, he finds that he can quash the danger or prevent it from arising, surely he has the right to do this too. Thus, Hammarskjöld felt that the Charter entitled him to set the United Nations machinery in motion on his own authority, even before he had a mandate from the Security Council and the General Assembly. It implied "a broad discretion to conduct inquiries and to engage in formal diplomatic activities in regard to matters which may threaten the maintenance of international peace and security"; or it permitted the use of his "good offices to prevent situations from developing."*

Since some Members maintained that the Secretary-General was merely "the chief administrative officer" of the Secretariat, this led to the accusation of "usurpation of power." Soviet Foreign Minister Andrei Gromyko called Hammarskjöld a "United Nations Field Marshal," and suspected that he regarded himself as the "Prime Minister of a World Government." In replying to these accusations the Secretary-General permitted himself some rare sarcasm: "It is a common experience to everyone who has tried to pursue a line of independence and objectivity in human affairs that he comes under criticism from those who believe that they would have had a greater chance of success for their own special aims if it had not been for his attitude.

"The responsibility of the Secretary-General under the Charter cannot be laid aside merely because the execution of decisions by him is likely to be politically controversial. The Secretary-General remains under obligation to carry out the policies as adopted by the organs. The essential requirement is that he does this on the basis of his exclusively international responsibility and not in the interest of any particular State or groups of States."

⟪ According to the Charter, the Secretary-General has no special authority to, so to say, settle conflicts. He has been given one instrument and that is the right, himself, to appeal to the Security Council where there is a threat to peace and security. That instrument is a somewhat violent and dramatic one. It is a kind of political H-bomb, and for that reason, it has more importance in principle than it can possibly have in practice. [4]

⟪ Very many Member nations have not yet accepted the limits put on their national ambitions by the very existence of the United Nations and by the membership of that Organization. [55]

⟪ A passive acceptance of a nationalism rendering it necessary to abandon present efforts in the direction of internationalism symbolized by the international civil service . . . might, if accepted by the Member nations, well prove to be the Munich of international cooperation as conceived after the First World War and further developed under the impression of the tragedy of the Second World War. To abandon or to compromise with principles on which such cooperation is built may be no less dangerous than to compromise with principles regarding the rights of a nation. In both cases the price to be paid may be peace. [56]

⟨ This organization is too often and too easily used as a whipping horse by those who wish to unburden themselves of their own responsibilities; this organization which, however, represents values and hopes which go beyond that of any single man, any single political group, and—why not—any single country. [54]

⟨ We countered effectively efforts from all sides to make the Congo a happy hunting ground for national interests. To be a road block to such efforts is to make yourself the target of attacks from all those who find their plans thwarted. [55]

⟨ If integrity in the sense of respect for law and respect for truth were to drive him into positions of conflict with this or that interest, then that conflict is a sign of his neutrality and not of his failure to observe neutrality—then it is in line, not in conflict, with his duties as an international civil servant. [56]

⟨ The principles of the Charter are, by far, greater than the Organization in which they are embodied, and the aims which they are to safeguard are holier than the policies of any single nation or people. As a servant of the Organization the Secretary-General has the duty to maintain his usefulness by avoiding public stands on conflicts between Member nations unless and until such an action might help to resolve the conflict. However, the discretion and impartiality thus imposed on the Secretary-General by the character of his immediate task may not degenerate into a policy of expediency. He must also be a servant of the principles of the Charter, and its aims must ultimately determine what for him is right and wrong. For that he must stand. [33]

❨ Mr. Krishna Menon, in his speech the other day, made the important point that changing situations may call for a change in reactions; what the Secretary-General said several months ago, as he stated, may not be what he would say today. I certainly agree with this pragmatic attitude as long as it is not a question of principles. [68]

Among the most significant statements ever made by Hammarskjöld was his reply in the fall of 1960 to the Soviet Union's repeated attacks on him for his conduct of the Congo operations. While refraining from defending himself against purely personal attacks, the Secretary-General laid forth his belief in the United Nations as a forum for small powers and in the principles of the Organization as being greater than its individual members.

During the fifteenth session of the General Assembly, on September 23, 1960, Chairman Nikita S. Khrushchev came forward with his famous "troika" proposal. The Secretary-General's office, he said, should be replaced by an executive body "comprising three persons, each of whom would represent a certain group of states, that is to say, the Western states, the Communist, and the nonaligned." To this Hammarskjöld replied as follows.

❨ Time and again the United Nations has had to face situations in which a wrong move might have tended to throw the weight of the Organization over in favor of this or that specific party in a conflict of a primarily domestic character. To permit that to happen is indeed to intervene in domestic affairs contrary to the letter and the spirit of the Charter.

Use whatever words you like, independence, impartiality, objectivity—they all describe essential aspects of what, without exception, must be the attitude of the Secretary-General. Such an attitude . . . may at any stage become an obstacle for those who work for certain political aims which would be better served or more easily achieved if the Secretary-General compromised with this attitude. But if he did how gravely he would then betray the trust of all those for whom the strict maintenance of such an attitude is their best protection in the world-wide fight for power and influence. Thus, if the office of the Secretary-General becomes a stumbling block for anyone, be it an individual, a group, or a government, because the incumbent stands by the basic principle which must guide his whole activity, and if, for that reason, he comes under criticism, such criticism strikes at the very office and the concepts on which it is based. I would rather see that office break on strict adherence to the principle of independence, impartiality, and objectivity than drift on the basis of compromise. [52]

On October 3 Khrushchev returned to the fray, accusing Hammarskjöld of being biased against the socialist countries and of using the United Nations in support of the colonial powers; he warned that if he "does not muster enough courage to resign, so to say in a chivalrous manner, then the Soviet Union will draw the necessary conclusions. . . ."

The same afternoon, Hammarskjöld gave his answer.

The General Assembly can rightly expect an immediate reply from my side to a statement so directly addressed to me and regarding a matter of such potential significance.

The Assembly has witnessed over the last weeks how historical truth is established; once an allegation has been repeated a few times, it is no longer an allegation, it is an established fact, even if no evidence has been brought out in order to support it. However, facts are facts, and the true facts are there for whosoever cares for truth. Those who invoke history will certainly be heard by history. And they will have to accept its verdict as it will be pronounced on the basis of the facts by men free of mind and firm in their conviction that only on a scrutiny of truth can a future of peace be built.

I regret that the intervention to which I have found it necessary to reply has again tended to personalize an issue which, as I have said, in my view is not a question of a man but of an institution. The man does not count, the institution does. A weak or nonexistent executive would mean that the United Nations would no longer be able to serve as an effective instrument for active protection of the interests of those many Members who need such protection. The man holding the responsibility as chief executive should leave if he weakens the executive; he should stay if this is necessary for its maintenance. This, and only this, seems to me to be substantive criterion that has to be applied.

The statement this morning seems to indicate that the Soviet Union finds it impossible to work with the present Secretary-General. This may seem to provide a strong reason why I should resign. However, the Soviet Union has also made it clear that, if the present Secretary-General were to resign now, they would not wish to elect a new incumbent but insist on an arrangement which—and this is my firm conviction based on broad experience —would make it impossible to maintain an effective executive. By resigning, I would, therefore, at the present difficult and dangerous juncture throw the Organization to the winds. I have no right to do so because I have a responsibility to all those States Members for which the Organization is of decisive importance, a responsibility which overrides all other considerations.

It is not the Soviet Union or, indeed, any other Big Powers who need the United Nations for their protection; it is all the others. In this sense the Organization is first of all *their* Organization, and I deeply believe in the wisdom with which they will be able to use it and guide it. I shall remain in my post during the term of my office as a servant of the Organization in the interests of all those other nations, as long as *they* wish me to do so.

In this context the representative of the Soviet Union spoke of courage. It is very easy to resign; it is not so easy to stay on. It is very easy to bow to the wish of a Big Power. It is another matter to resist. As is well known to all members of this Assembly, I have done so before on many occasions and in many directions. If it is the wish of those nations who see in the Organization their best protection in the present world, I shall now do so again. [53]

❨ It is my firm conviction that any result bought at the price of a compromise with the principles and ideals of the Organization, either by yielding to force, by disregard of justice, by neglect of common interests, or by contempt for human rights, is bought at too high a price. That is so because a compromise with its principles and purposes weakens the Organization in a way representing a definite loss for the future that cannot be balanced by any immediate advantage achieved. [18]

❨ We have been accused of servility in relation to the West, of softness in relation to the East, of supporting this or that man in the Congo whom one group or another on the world scene has chosen to make its symbol, or for assisting another man to whom another group has chosen to tie their hopes for the success of interest they wish to safeguard. However, this is no excessive price to be paid for avoiding the thing for which no one in my position should be forgiven: to compromise, in any political interest, with the aims and principles of this Organization. It has not been done and it will not be done with my knowledge or acquiescence. I can only repeat what I said in the General Assembly, that I would rather like to see the office of the Secretary-General break on this principle than drift on a compromise. [54]

❨ Responsibility is not a question of political terminology or rhetoric. It is a question of fact and if the facts are not seen now they all the same will remain on the record. [68]

❨ The main accusations against the Secretary-General that he has acted in accordance with requests for which the accusers have voted. [74]

After the murder of Patrice Lumumba in February, 1961, Valerian Zorin, the representative of the USSR, addressed a letter to the President of the Security Council in which he declared: "The blood of Patrice Lumumba is on the hands of this henchman of the colonialists and cannot be removed." Thereafter, the Soviet Union, followed by other Communist nations, refused to recognize Hammarskjöld as an official of the United Nations.

On June 26, 1961, three months before his death, at a press conference at United Nations Headquarters, Hammarskjöld was asked:

QUESTION: How do you run a "troika" without a coachman?

THE SECRETARY-GENERAL: Well, I have never tried a "troika" and I do not think I ever will. [61]

39

His Legacy

In the summer of 1961, immediately before leaving for the Congo and his death, Hammarskjöld prepared and signed his annual report to the General Assembly.

His introduction (Source 19) may be looked upon as his political testament. Although it is written in his usual impersonal tone, one feels the beat of his bitter experiences of the previous months. He repeats with emphasis his main views about disarmament, human rights, and the rule of law, and continues with a stern analysis of the political philosophy prevalent among Member nations.

*Some Members, he wrote, conceive of a World Organization whose aim does not go beyond peaceful coexistence. It is a con-*ference machinery *for resolving conflicts of interest and ideology* with a Secretariat not fully internationalized, but representing *within its ranks the same interests and ideologies. The situation is static, admitting no development of the Organization.*

He juxtaposed this concept against another: that of an Organization which is a dynamic instrument *of governments through which they might not only seek reconciliation and coexistence, but also develop forms of executive action in order to forestall conflicts and resolve them. This Organization is served by a fully internationalized Secretariat, the actions of whose Members are guided solely by the principles of the Charter, the decisions of the main organs, and the interests of the Organization itself.*

The first concept is "firmly anchored in the time-honored philosophy of sovereign national states in armed competition. . . . The second one envisages . . . opening the road toward more developed and increasingly effective forms of constructive international cooperation."

Hammarskjöld perceived that the choice between the conflicting views ran through the entire fabric of the United Nations, and in his testament he examined how it effected the thinking and actions of nations in many different fields of activity. He ended his report with these words: "The Organization has now reached a stage in its development where Member nations may find it timely to clarify their views on the direction in whch they would like to see the future work of the Organization develop."

⟨[The growth of the United Nations out of the historic conference pattern—at all events naturally remains the starting point in all efforts of the Organization—is clearly reflected in what, in the light of experience, may seem to be a lack of balance in the Charter. While great attention is given to the principles and purposes, and considerable space is devoted to an elaboration of what may be called the parliamentary aspects of the Organization, little is said about executive arrangements.

While the Organization, if regarded as a standing diplomatic conference, might well be serviced by a fully international Secretariat but does not need it, the other approach to the Organization and its role cannot be satisfied with anything less than a Secretariat of an exclusively international character, and thus cannot be reconciled with a Secretariat composed on party lines and on the assumption that the interests represented in the main organs in this manner should be represented and advocated also within the Secretariat. Thus, again, the choice between conflicting views on the United Nations Secretariat is basically a choice between conflicting views on the Organization, its functions, and its future.

In the traditional conference pattern, participants in a meeting are mostly serviced by a Secretariat drawn from the same countries as the participants themselves, and constituting a mixed group regarding which there is no need to demand or maintain an exclusively international character.

The discussion regarding the development of executive functions is basically one confronting the same fundamentally different concepts of the Organization and its place in international politics, which could be seen also in the different attitudes toward the legal weight of decisions of the Organization.

For those who maintain the conference concept of the Organization, it is natural to side step the mandatory nature of decisions by the Security Council. For those who take a different view, it is equally natural and essential to work for a full and general acceptance of the Charter rules.

[Although] the decisions of the Assembly have, as regards Member States, only the character of recommendations [and they], legally, are only recommendations, they introduce an important element by expressing a majority consensus on the issue under consideration.

Naturally, such a formula leaves scope for a gradual development in practice of the weight of the decisions. To the extent that more respect, in fact, is shown to General Assembly recommendations by the Member States, they may come more and more close to being recognized as decisions having a binding effect on those concerned, particularly when they involve the application of the binding principles of the Charter and of international law.

It is in conflicts relating to the development toward full self-government and independence that the Organization has faced its most complicated tasks in the executive field. It is also in the case of executive action in this context that different concepts of the

Organization and of its decisions and structure have their most pointed expressions.

The character of the mandates has, in many cases, been such that in carrying out his functions the Secretary-General has found himself forced also to interpret the decisions in the light of the Charter, United Nations precedents, and the aims and intentions expressed by the members. When that has been the case, the Secretary-General has been under the obligation to seek guidance, to all possible extent, from the main organs; but when such guidance has not been forthcoming, developments have sometimes led to situations in which he has had to shoulder responsibility for certain limited political functions.

This whole development has lately become a matter of controversy, natural and, indeed, unavoidable in the light of differences of approach to the role of the Organization. . . . While the development is welcomed by Member nations which feel a need of growth as regards the possibilities of the Organization to engage in executive action in protection of the Charter principles, it is rejected by those who maintain the conference concept of the Organization.

So far, the economic and technical activities of the United Nations have been less influenced by the conflict between different concepts of the role of the Organization than its activities in other fields. However, it is impossible to isolate the economic and technical problems from the general question discussed in this introduction.

Again, the problem arises in the basic concept of the United Nations. With the conference approach to the work of the Organization a choice is made also in favor of bilateral assistance, while the alternative approach opens the door to a development under which international assistance, in implementation of the principle of equal economic opportunities for all, would be channeled through the Organization or its related agencies. . . .

The effort through the Organization to find a way by which the world community might, step by step, grow into organized international cooperation within the Charter must either progress or recede. Those whose reactions to the work of the Organization hamper its development or reduce its possibilities of effective action may have to shoulder the responsibility for a return to a state of affairs which governments had already found too dangerous after the First World War.

[*Hammarskjöld did not present his report to the Assembly in person. The day before the Assembly convened he died in a plane crash in the Ndola forest.*]

NOTE

Amendments to Articles 23, 27 and 61 of the Charter of the United Nations, adopted by the General Assembly on 17 December 1963, came into force on 31 August 1965. An amendment to Article 109, adopted by the General Assembly on 20 December 1965, is in the process of ratification by Member States.

The amendment to Article 23 enlarges the membership of the Security Council from eleven to fifteen.

The amended Article 27 provides that decisions of the Security Council on procedural matters shall be made by an affirmative vote of nine members (formerly seven) and on all other matters by an affirmative vote of nine members (formerly seven), including the concurring votes of the five permanent members of the Security Council.

The amendment to Article 61 enlarges the membership of the Economic and Social Council from eighteen to twenty-seven.

The amendment to Article 109 provides that a General Conference of Member States for the purpose of reviewing the Charter may be held at a date and place to be fixed by a two-thirds vote of the members of the General Assembly and by a vote of any nine members (formerly seven) of the Security Council.

Charter of the United Nations

WE THE PEOPLES OF THE UNITED NATIONS DETERMINED

to save succeeding generations from the scourge of war, which twice in our lifetime has brought untold sorrow to mankind, and

to reaffirm faith in fundamental human rights, in the dignity and worth of the human person, in the equal rights of men and women and of nations large and small, and

to establish conditions under which justice and respect for the obligations arising from treaties and other sources of international law can be maintained, and

to promote social progress and better standards of life in larger freedom,

AND FOR THESE ENDS

to practice tolerance and live together in peace with one another as good neighbors, and

to unite our strength to maintain international peace and security, and

to ensure, by the acceptance of principles and the institution of methods, that armed force shall not be used, save in the common interest, and

to employ international machinery for the promotion of the economic and social advancement of all peoples,

HAVE RESOLVED TO COMBINE OUR EFFORTS TO ACCOMPLISH
THESE AIMS.

Accordingly, our respective Governments, through representatives
assembled in the city of San Francisco, who have exhibited their
full powers found to be in good and due form, have agreed to the
present Charter of the United Nations and do hereby establish
an international organization to be known as the United Nations.

CHAPTER 1

Purposes and Principles

ARTICLE 1

The Purposes of the United Nations are:

1. To maintain international peace and security, and to that end: to
take effective collective measures for the prevention and removal of
threats to the peace, and for the suppression of acts of aggression or
other breaches of the peace, and to bring about by peaceful means,
and in conformity with the principles of justice and international law,
adjustment or settlement of international disputes or situations which
might lead to a breach of the peace;

2. To develop friendly relations among nations based on respect for
the principle of equal rights and self-determination of peoples, and to
take other appropriate measures to strengthen universal peace;

3. To achieve international cooperation in solving international
problems of an economic, social, cultural, or humanitarian character,
and in promoting and encouraging respect for human rights and for
fundamental freedoms for all without distinction as to race, sex, language, or religion; and

4. To be a center for harmonizing the actions of nations in the
attainment of these common ends.

ARTICLE 2

The Organization and its Members, in pursuit of the Purposes stated
in Article 1, shall act in accordance with the following Principles.

1. The Organization is based on the principle of the sovereign
equality of all its Members.

2. All Members, in order to ensure to all of them the rights and
benefits resulting from membership, shall fulfil in good faith the obli-

gations assumed by them in accordance with the present Charter.

3. All Members shall settle their international disputes by peaceful means in such a manner that international peace and security, and justice, are not endangered.

4. All Members shall refrain in their international relations from the threat or use of force against the territorial integrity or political independence of any state, or in any other manner inconsistent with the Purposes of the United Nations.

5. All Members shall give the United Nations every assistance in any action it takes in accordance with the present Charter, and shall refrain from giving assistance to any state against which the United Nations is taking preventive or enforcement action.

6. The Organization shall ensure that states which are not Members of the United Nations act in accordance with these Principles so far as may be necessary for the maintenance of international peace and security.

7. Nothing contained in the present Charter shall authorize the United Nations to intervene in matters which are essentially within the domestic jurisdiction of any state or shall require the Members to submit such matters to settlement under the present Charter; but this principle shall not prejudice the application of enforcement measures under Chapter 7.

CHAPTER 2

Membership

ARTICLE 3

The original Members of the United Nations shall be the states which, having participated in the United Nations Conference on International Organization at San Francisco, or having previously signed the Declaration by United Nations of January 1, 1942, sign the present Charter and ratify it in accordance with Article 110.

ARTICLE 4

1. Membership in the United Nations is open to all other peace-loving states which accept the obligations contained in the present Charter and, in the judgment of the Organization, are able and willing to carry out these obligations.

2. The admission of any such state to membership in the United Nations will be effected by a decision of the General Assembly upon the recommendation of the Security Council.

A R T I C L E 5

A Member of the United Nations against which preventive or enforcement action has been taken by the Security Council may be suspended from the exercise of the rights and privileges of membership by the General Assembly upon the recommendation of the Security Council. The exercise of these rights and privileges may be restored by the Security Council.

A R T I C L E 6

A Member of the United Nations which has persistently violated the Principles contained in the present Charter may be expelled from the Organization by the General Assembly upon the recommendation of the Security Council.

C H A P T E R 3

Organs

A R T I C L E 7

1. There are established as the principal organs of the United Nations: a General Assembly, a Security Council, an Economic and Social Council, a Trusteeship Council, an International Court of Justice, and a Secretariat.

2. Such subsidiary organs as may be found necessary may be established in accordance with the present Charter.

A R T I C L E 8

The United Nations shall place no restrictions on the eligibility of men and women to participate in any capacity and under conditions of equality in its principal and subsidiary organs.

CHAPTER 4

The General Assembly

Composition

ARTICLE 9

1. The General Assembly shall consist of all the Members of the United Nations.

2. Each Member shall have not more than five representatives in the General Assembly.

Functions and Powers

ARTICLE 10

The General Assembly may discuss any questions or any matters within the scope of the present Charter or relating to the powers and functions of any organs provided for in the present Charter, and except as provided in Article 12, may make recommendations to the Members of the United Nations or to the Security Council or to both on any such questions or matters.

ARTICLE 11

1. The General Assembly may consider the general principles of cooperation in the maintenance of international peace and security, including the principles governing disarmament and the regulation of armaments, and may make recommendations with regard to such principles to the Members or to the Security Council or to both.

2. The General Assembly may discuss any questions relating to the maintenance of international peace and security brought before it by any Member of the United Nations, or by the Security Council, or by a state which is not a Member of the United Nations in accordance with Article 35, paragraph 2, and, except as provided in Article 12, may make recommendations with regard to any such questions to the state or states concerned or to the Security Council or to both. Any such question on which action is necessary shall be referred to the Security Council by the General Assembly either before or after discussion.

3. The General Assembly may call the attention of the Security

Council to situations which are likely to endanger international peace and security.

4. The powers of the General Assembly set forth in this Article shall not limit the general scope of Article 10.

ARTICLE 12

1. While the Security Council is exercising in respect of any dispute or situation the functions assigned to it in the present Charter, the General Assembly shall not make any recommendation with regard to that dispute or situation unless the Security Council so requests.

2. The Secretary-General, with the consent of the Security Council, shall notify the General Assembly at each session of any matters relative to the maintenance of international peace and security which are being dealt with by the Security Council and shall similarly notify the General Assembly, or the Members of the United Nations if the General Assembly is not in session, immediately the Security Council ceases to deal with such matters.

ARTICLE 13

1. The General Assembly shall initiate studies and make recommendations for the purpose of:

a. promoting international cooperation in the political field and encouraging the progressive development of international law and its codification;

b. promoting international cooperation in the economic, social, cultural, educational, and health fields, and assisting in the realization of human rights and fundamental freedoms for all without distinction as to race, sex, language, or religion.

2. The further responsibilities, functions, and powers of the General Assembly with respect to matters mentioned in paragraph 1 (b) above are set forth in Chapters 9 and 10.

ARTICLE 14

Subject to the provisions of Article 12, the General Assembly may recommend measures for the peaceful adjustment of any situation, regardless of origin, which it deems likely to impair the general welfare or friendly relations among nations, including situations resulting from a violation of the provisions of the present Charter setting forth the Purposes and Principles of the United Nations.

A R T I C L E 1 5

1. The General Assembly shall receive and consider annual and special reports from the Security Council; these reports shall include an account of the measures that the Security Council has decided upon or taken to maintain international peace and security.

2. The General Assembly shall receive and consider reports from the other organs of the United Nations.

A R T I C L E 1 6

The General Assembly shall perform such functions with respect to the international trusteeship system as are assigned to it under Chapters 12 and 13, including the approval of the trusteeship agreements for areas not designated as strategic.

A R T I C L E 1 7

1. The General Assembly shall consider and approve the budget of the Organization.

2. The expenses of the Organization shall be borne by the Members as apportioned by the General Assembly.

3. The General Assembly shall consider and approve any financial and budgetary arrangements with specialized agencies referred to in Article 57 and shall examine the administrative budgets of such specialized agencies with a view to making recommendations to the agencies concerned.

Voting

A R T I C L E 1 8

1. Each member of the General Assembly shall have one vote.

2. Decisions of the General Assembly on important questions shall be made by a two-thirds majority of the members present and voting. These questions shall include: recommendations with respect to the maintenance of international peace and security, the election of the non-permanent members of the Security Council, the election of the members of the Economic and Social Council, the election of members of the Trusteeship Council in accordance with paragraph 1 (c) of Article 86, the admission of new Members to the United Nations, the suspension of the rights and privileges of membership, the expulsion of

Members, questions relating to the operation of the trusteeship system, and budgetary questions.

3. Decisions on other questions, including the determination of additional categories of questions to be decided by a two-thirds majority, shall be made by a majority of the members present and voting.

ARTICLE 19

A member of the United Nations which is in arrears in the payment of its financial contributions to the Organization shall have no vote in the General Assembly if the amount of its arrears equals or exceeds the amount of the contributions due from it for the preceding two full years. The General Assembly may, nevertheless, permit such a Member to vote if it is satisfied that the failure to pay is due to conditions beyond the control of the Member.

Procedure

ARTICLE 20

The General Assembly shall meet in regular annual sessions and in such special sessions as occasion may require. Special sessions shall be convoked by the Secretary-General at the request of the Security Council or of a majority of the Members of the United Nations.

ARTICLE 21

The General Assembly shall adopt its own rules of procedure. It shall elect its President for each session.

ARTICLE 22

The General Assembly may establish such subsidiary organs as it deems necessary for the performance of its functions.

CHAPTER 5

The Security Council

Composition

ARTICLE 23

1. The Security Council shall consist of eleven* Members of the United Nations. The Republic of China, France, the Union of Soviet

*See Note, p. 192.

Socialist Republics, the United Kingdom of Great Britain and Northern Ireland, and the United States of America shall be permanent members of the Security Council. The General Assembly shall elect six other Members of the United Nations to be non-permanent members of the Security Council, due regard being specially paid, in the first instance to the contribution of Members of the United Nations to the maintenance of international peace and security and to the other purposes of the Organization, and also to equitable geographical distribution.

2. The non-permanent members of the Security Council shall be elected for a term of two years. In the first election of the non-permanent members, however, three shall be chosen for a term of one year. A retiring member shall not be eligible for immediate re-election.

3. Each member of the Security Council shall have one representative.

Functions and Powers

A R T I C L E 2 4

1. In order to ensure prompt and effective action by the United Nations, its Members confer on the Security Council primary responsibility for the maintenance of international peace and security, and agree that in carrying out its duties under this responsibility the Security Council acts on their behalf.

2. In discharging these duties the Security Council shall act in accordance with the Purposes and Principles of the United Nations. The specific powers granted to the Security Council for the discharge of these duties are laid down in Chapters 6, 7, 8, and 12.

3. The Security Council shall submit annual and, when necessary, special reports to the General Assembly for its consideration.

A R T I C L E 2 5

The Members of the United Nations agree to accept and carry out the decisions of the Security Council in accordance with the present Charter.

A R T I C L E 2 6

In order to promote the establishment and maintenance of international peace and security with the least diversion for armaments of the world's human and economic resources, the Security Council shall be responsible for formulating, with the assistance of the Military Staff Committee referred to in Article 47, plans to be submitted to the Members of the United Nations for the establishment of a system for the regulation of armaments.

Voting

ARTICLE 27

1. Each member of the Security Council shall have one vote.

2. Decisions of the Security Council on procedural matters shall be made by an affirmative vote of seven* members.

3. Decisions of the Security Council on all other matters shall be made by an affirmative vote of seven* members including the concurring votes of the permanent members; provided that, in decisions under Chapter 6, and under paragraph 3 of Article 52, a party to a dispute shall abstain from voting.

Procedure

ARTICLE 28

1. The Security Council shall be so organized as to be able to function continuously. Each member of the Security Council shall for this purpose be represented at all times at the seat of the Organization.

2. The Security Council shall hold periodic meetings at which each of its members may, if it so desires, be represented by a member of the government or by some other specially designated representative.

3. The Security Council may hold meetings at such places other than the seat of the Organization as in its judgment will best facilitate its work.

ARTICLE 29

The Security Council may establish such subsidiary organs as it deems necessary for the performance of its functions.

ARTICLE 30

The Security Council shall adopt its own rules of procedure, including the method of selecting its President.

*See Note, p. 192.

A R T I C L E   3 1

Any Member of the United Nations which is not a member of the Security Council may participate, without vote, in the discussion of any question brought before the Security Council whenever the latter considers that the interests of that Member are specially affected.

A R T I C L E   3 2

Any Member of the United Nations which is not a member of the Security Council or any state which is not a Member of the United Nations, if it is a party to a dispute under consideration by the Security Council, shall be invited to participate, without vote, in the discussion relating to the dispute. The Security Council shall lay down such conditions as it deems just for the participation of a state which is not a Member of the United Nations.

C H A P T E R   6

Pacific Settlement of Disputes

A R T I C L E   3 3

1. The parties to any dispute, the continuance of which is likely to endanger the maintenance of international peace and security, shall, first of all, seek a solution by negotiation, enquiry, mediation, conciliation, arbitration, judicial settlement, resort to regional agencies or arrangements, or other peaceful means of their own choice.

2. The Security Council shall, when it deems necessary, call upon the parties to settle their dispute by such means.

A R T I C L E   3 4

The Security Council may investigate any dispute, or any situation which might lead to international friction or give rise to a dispute, in order to determine whether the continuance of the dispute or situation is likely to endanger the maintenance of international peace and security.

A R T I C L E   3 5

1. Any Member of the United Nations may bring any dispute, or any situation of the nature referred to in Article 34, to the attention of the Security Council or of the General Assembly.

2. A state which is not a Member of the United Nations may bring to the attention of the Security Council or of the General Assembly any dispute to which it is a party if it accepts in advance, for the purposes of the dispute, the obligations of pacific settlement provided in the present Charter.

3. The proceedings of the General Assembly in respect of matters brought to its attention under this Article will be subject to the provisions of Articles 11 and 12.

ARTICLE 36

1. The Security Council may, at any stage of a dispute of the nature referred to in Article 33 or of a situation of like nature, recommend appropriate procedures or methods of adjustment.

2. The Security Council should take into consideration any procedures for the settlement of the dispute which have already been adopted by the parties.

3. In making recommendations under this Article the Security Council should also take into consideration that legal disputes should as a general rule be referred by the parties to the International Court of Justice in accordance with the provisions of the Statute of the Court.

ARTICLE 37

1. Should the parties to a dispute of the nature referred to in Article 33 fail to settle it by the means indicated in that Article, they shall refer it to the Security Council.

2. If the Security Council deems that the continuance of the dispute is in fact likely to endanger the maintenance of international peace and security, it shall decide whether to take action under Article 36 or to recommend such terms of settlement as it may consider appropriate.

ARTICLE 38

Without prejudice to the provisions of Articles 33 to 37, the Security Council may, if all the parties to any dispute so request, make recommendations to the parties with a view to a pacific settlement of the dispute.

C H A P T E R   7

Action with Respect to Threats to the Peace, Breaches of the Peace, and Acts of Aggression

A R T I C L E   3 9

The Security Council shall determine the existence of any threat to the peace, breach of the peace, or act of aggression and shall make recommendations, or decide what measures shall be taken in accordance with Articles 41 and 42, to maintain or restore international peace and security.

A R T I C L E   4 0

In order to prevent an aggravation of the situation, the Security Council may, before making the recommendations or deciding upon the measures provided for in Article 39, call upon the parties concerned to comply with such provisional measures as it deems necesssary or desirable. Such provisional measures shall be without prejudice to the rights, claims, or position of the parties concerned. The Security Council shall duly take account of failure to comply with such provisional measures.

A R T I C L E   4 1

The Security Council may decide what measures not involving the use of armed force are to be employed to give effect to its decisions, and it may call upon the Members of the United Nations to apply such measures. These may include complete or partial interruption of economic relations and of rail, sea, air, postal, telegraphic, radio, and other means of communication, and the severance of diplomatic relations.

A R T I C L E   4 2

Should the Security Council consider that measures provided for in Article 41 would be inadequate or have proved to be inadequate, it may take such action by air, sea, or land forces as may be necessary to maintain or restore international peace and security. Such action may include demonstrations, blockade, and other operations by air, sea, or land forces of Members of the United Nations.

ARTICLE 43

1. All Members of the United Nations, in order to contribute to the maintenance of international peace and security, undertake to make available to the Security Council, on its call and in accordance with a special agreement or agreements, armed forces, assistance, and facilities, including rights of passage, necessary for the purpose of maintaining international peace and security.

2. Such agreement or agreements shall govern the numbers and types of forces, their degree of readiness and general location, and the nature of the facilities and assistance to be provided.

3. The agreement or agreements shall be negotiated as soon as possible on the initiative of the Security Council. They shall be concluded between the Security Council and Members or between the Security Council and groups of Members and shall be subject to ratification by the signatory states in accordance with their respective constitutional processes.

ARTICLE 44

When the Security Council has decided to use force it shall, before calling upon a Member not represented on it to provide armed forces in fulfillment of the obligations assumed under Article 43, invite that Member, if the Member so desires, to participate in the decisions of the Security Council concerning the employment of contingents of that Member's armed forces.

ARTICLE 45

In order to enable the United Nations to take urgent military measures, Members shall hold immediately available national air-force contingents for combined international enforcement action. The strength and degree of readiness of these contingents and plans for their combined action shall be determined, within the limits laid down in the special agreement or agreements referred to in Article 43, by the Security Council with the assistance of the Military Staff Committee.

ARTICLE 46

Plans for the application of armed force shall be made by the Security Council with the assistance of the Military Staff Committee.

A R T I C L E 4 7

1. There shall be established a Military Staff Committee to advise and assist the Security Council on all questions relating to the Security Council's military requirements for the maintenance of international peace and security, the employment and command of forces placed at its disposal, the regulation of armaments, and possible disarmament.

2. The Military Staff Committee shall consist of the Chiefs of Staff of the permanent members of the Security Council or their representatives. Any Member of the United Nations not permanently represented on the Committee shall be invited by the Committee to be associated with it when the efficient discharge of the Committee's responsibilities requires the participation of that Member in its work.

3. The Military Staff Committee shall be responsible under the Security Council for the strategic direction of any armed forces placed at the disposal of the Security Council. Questions relating to the command of such forces shall be worked out subsequently.

4. The Military Staff Committee, with the authorization of the Security Council and after consultation with appropriate regional agencies, may establish regional subcommittees.

A R T I C L E 4 8

1. The action required to carry out the decisions of the Security Council for the maintenance of international peace and security shall be taken by all the Members of the United Nations or by some of them, as the Security Council may determine.

2. Such decisions shall be carried out by the Members of the United Nations directly and through their action in the appropriate international agencies of which they are members.

A R T I C L E 4 9

The Members of the United Nations shall join in affording mutual assistance in carrying out the measures decided upon by the Security Council.

A R T I C L E 5 0

If preventive or enforcement measures against any state are taken by the Security Council, any other state, whether a Member of the United Nations or not, which finds itself confronted with special economic problems arising from the carrying out of those measures shall have the right to consult the Security Council with regard to a solution of those problems.

ARTICLE 51

Nothing in the present Charter shall impair the inherent right of individual or collective self-defense if an armed attack occurs against a Member of the United Nations, until the Security Council has taken the measures necessary to maintain international peace and security. Measures taken by Members in the exercise of this right of self-defense shall be immediately reported to the Security Council and shall not in any way affect the authority and responsibility of the Security Council under the present Charter to take at any time such action as it deems necessary in order to maintain or restore international peace and security.

CHAPTER 8

Regional Arrangements

ARTICLE 52

1. Nothing in the present Charter precludes the existence of regional arrangements or agencies for dealing with such matters relating to the maintenance of international peace and security as are appropriate for regional action, provided that such arrangements or agencies and their activities are consistent with the Purposes and Principles of the United Nations.

2. The Members of the United Nations entering into such arrangements or constituting such agencies shall make every effort to achieve pacific settlement of local disputes through such regional arrangements or by such regional agencies before referring them to the Security Council.

3. The Security Council shall encourage the development of pacific settlement of local disputes through such regional arrangements or by such regional agencies either on the initiative of the states concerned or by reference from the Security Council.

4. This Article is no way impairs the application of Articles 34 and 35.

A R T I C L E   5 3

1. The Security Council shall, where appropriate, utilize such regional arrangements or agencies for enforcement action under its authority. But no enforcement action shall be taken under regional arrangements or by regional agencies without the authorization of the Security Council, with the exception of measures against any enemy state, as defined in paragraph 2 of this Article, provided for pursuant to Article 107 or in regional arrangements directed against renewal of aggressive policy on the part of any such state, until such time as the Organization may, on request of the Governments concerned, be charged with the responsibility for preventing further aggression by such a state.

2. The term enemy state as used in paragraph 1 of this Article applies to any state which during the Second World War has been an enemy of any signatory of the present Charter.

A R T I C L E   5 4

The Security Council shall at all times be kept fully informed of activities undertaken or in contemplation under regional arrangements or by regional agencies for the maintenance of international peace and security.

C H A P T E R   9

International Economic and Social Cooperation

A R T I C L E   5 5

With a view to the creation of conditions of stability and well-being which are necessary for peaceful and friendly relations among nations based on respect for the principle of equal rights and self-determination of peoples, the United Nations shall promote:

a. higher standards of living, full employment, and conditions of economic and social progress and development;

b. solutions of international economic, social, health, and related problems; and international cultural and educational cooperation; and

c. universal respect for, and observance of, human rights and fundamental freedoms for all without distinction as to race, sex, language, or religion.

ARTICLE 56

All Members pledge themselves to take joint and separate action in cooperation with the Organization for the achievement of the purposes set forth in Article 55.

ARTICLE 57

1. The various specialized agencies, established by intergovernmental agreement and having wide international responsibilities, as defined in their basic instruments, in economic, social, cultural, educational, health, and related fields, shall be brought into relationship with the United Nations in accordance with the provisions of Article 63.

2. Such agencies thus brought into relationship with the United Nations are hereinafter referred to as specialized agencies.

ARTICLE 58

The Organization shall make recommendations for the coordination of the policies and activities of the specialized agencies.

ARTICLE 59

The Organization shall, where appropriate, initiate negotiations among the states concerned for the creation of any new specialized agencies required for the accomplishment of the purposes set forth in Article 55.

ARTICLE 60

Responsibility for the discharge of the functions of the Organization set forth in this Chapter shall be vested in the General Assembly and, under the authority of the General Assembly, in the Economic and Social Council, which shall have for this purpose the powers set forth in Chapter 10.

CHAPTER 10

The Economic and Social Council

Composition

ARTICLE 61

1. The Economic and Social Council shall consist of eighteen* Members of the United Nations elected by the General Assembly.

*See Note, p. 192.

2. Subject to the provisions of paragraph 3, six members of the Economic and Social Council shall be elected each year for a term of three years. A retiring member shall be eligible for immediate re-election.

3. At the first election, eighteen members of the Economic and Social Council shall be chosen. The term of office of six members so chosen shall expire at the end of one year, and of six other members at the end of two years, in accordance with arrangements made by the General Assembly.

4. Each member of the Economic and Social Council shall have one representative.

Functions and Powers

ARTICLE 62

1. The Economic and Social Council may make or initiate studies and reports with respect to international economic, social, cultural, educational, health, and related matters and may make recommendations with respect to any such matters to the General Assembly, to the Members of the United Nations, and to the specialized agencies concerned.

2. It may make recommendations for the purpose of promoting respect for, and observance of, human rights and fundamental freedoms for all.

3. It may prepare draft conventions for submission to the General Assembly, with respect to matters falling within its competence.

4. It may call, in accordance with the rules prescribed by the United Nations, international conferences on matters falling within its competence.

ARTICLE 63

1. The Economic and Social Council may enter into agreements with any of the agencies referred to in Article 57, defining the terms on which the agency concerned shall be brought into relationship with the United Nations. Such agreements shall be subject to approval by the General Assembly.

2. It may coordinate the activities of the specialized agencies through consultation with and recommendations to such agencies and through recommendations to the General Assembly and to the Members of the United Nations.

ARTICLE 64

1. The Economic and Social Council may take appropriate steps to obtain regular reports from the specialized agencies. It may make arrangements with the Members of the United Nations and with the specialized agencies to obtain reports on the steps taken to give effect to its own recommendations and to recommendations on matters falling within its competence made by the General Assembly.

2. It may communicate its observations on these reports to the General Assembly.

ARTICLE 65

The Economic and Social Council may furnish information to the Security Council and shall assist the Security Council upon its request.

ARTICLE 66

1. The Economic and Social Council shall perform such functions as fall within its competence in connection with the carrying out of the recommendations of the General Assembly.

2. It may, with the approval of the General Assembly, perform services at the request of Members of the United Nations and at the request of specialized agencies.

3. It shall perform such other functions as are specified elsewhere in the present Charter or as may be assigned to it by the General Assembly.

Voting

ARTICLE 67

1. Each member of the Economic and Social Council shall have one vote.

2. Decisions of the Economic and Social Council shall be made by a majority of the members present and voting.

Procedure

ARTICLE 68

The Economic and Social Council shall set up commissions in economic and social fields and for the promotion of human rights, and such other commissions as may be required for the performance of its functions.

A R T I C L E   6 9

The Economic and Social Council shall invite any Member of the United Nations to participate, without vote, in its deliberations on any matter of particular concern to that Member.

A R T I C L E   7 0

The Economic and Social Council may make arrangements for representatives of the specialized agencies to participate, without vote, in its deliberations and in those of the commissions established by it, and for its representatives to participate in the deliberations of the specialized agencies.

A R T I C L E   7 1

The Economic and Social Council may make suitable arrangements for consultation with non-governmental organizations which are concerned with matters within its competence. Such arrangements may be made with international organizations and, where appropriate, with national organizations after consultation with the Member of the United Nations concerned.

A R T I C L E   7 2

1. The Economic and Social Council shall adopt its own rules of procedure, including the method of selecting its President.

2. The Economic and Social Council shall meet as required in accordance with its rules, which shall include provision for the convening of meetings on the request of a majority of its members.

C H A P T E R   1 1

Declaration Regarding Non-Self-Governing Territories

A R T I C L E   7 3

Members of the United Nations which have or assume responsibilities for the administration of territories whose peoples have not yet attained a full measure of self-government recognize the principle that the interests of the inhabitants of these territories are paramount, and accept as a sacred trust the obligation to promote to the utmost, within the system of international peace and security established by the present Charter, the well-being of the inhabitants of these territories, and, to this end:

a. to ensure, with due respect for the culture of the peoples concerned, their political, economic, social, and educational advancement, their just treatment, and their protection against abuses;

b. to develop self-government, to take due account of the political aspirations of the peoples, and to assist them in the progressive development of their free political institutions, according to the particular circumstances of each territory and its peoples and their varying stages of advancement;

c. to further international peace and security;

d. to promote constructive measures of development, to encourage research, and to cooperate with one another and, when and where appropriate, with specialized international bodies with a view to the practical achievement of the social, economic, and scientific purposes set forth in this Article; and

e. to transmit regularly to the Secretary-General for information purposes, subject to such limitation as security and constitutional considerations may require, statistical and other information of a technical nature relating to economic, social, and educational conditions in the territories for which they are respectively responsible other than those territories to which Chapters 12 and 13 apply.

ARTICLE 74

Members of the United Nations also agree that their policy in respect of the territories to which this Chapter applies, no less than in respect of their metropolitan areas, must be based on the general principle of good-neighborliness, due account being taken of the interests and well-being of the rest of the world, in social, economic, and commercial matters.

CHAPTER 12

International Trusteeship System

ARTICLE 75

The United Nations shall establish under its authority an international trusteeship system for the administration and supervision of such territories as may be placed thereunder by subsequent individual agreements. These territories are hereinafter referred to as trust territories.

ARTICLE 76

The basic objectives of the trusteeship system, in accordance with the Purposes of the United Nations laid down in Article 1 of the present Charter, shall be:

a. to further international peace and security;

b. to promote the political, economic, social, and educational advancement of the inhabitants of the trust territories, and their progressive development towards self-government or independence as may be appropriate to the particular circumstances of each territory and its peoples and the freely expressed wishes of the peoples concerned, and as may be provided by the terms of each trusteeship agreement;

c. to encourage respect for human rights and for fundamental freedoms for all without distinction as to race, sex, language, or religion, and to encourage recognition of the interdependence of the peoples of the world; and

d. to ensure equal treatment in social, economic, and commercial matters for all Members of the United Nations and their nationals, and also equal treatment for the latter in the administration of justice, without prejudice to the attainment of the foregoing objectives and subject to the provisions of Article 80.

ARTICLE 77

1. The trusteeship system shall apply to such territories in the following categories as may be placed thereunder by means of trusteeship agreements:

a. territories now held under mandate;

b. territories which may be detached from enemy states as a result of the Second World War; and

c. territories voluntarily placed under the system by states responsible for their administration.

2. It will be a matter for subsequent agreement as to which territories in the foregoing categories will be brought under the trusteeship system and upon what terms.

ARTICLE 78

The trusteeship system shall not apply to territories which have become Members of the United Nations, relationship among which shall be based on respect for the principle of sovereign equality.

A R T I C L E 7 9

The terms of trusteeship for each territory to be placed under the trusteeship system, including any alteration or amendment, shall be agreed upon by the states directly concerned, including the mandatory power in the case of territories held under mandate by a Member of the United Nations, and shall be approved as provided for in Articles 83 and 85.

A R T I C L E 8 0

1. Except as may be agreed upon in individual trusteeship agreements, made under Articles 77, 79, and 81, placing each territory under the trusteeship system, and until such agreements have been concluded, nothing in this Chapter shall be construed in or of itself to alter in any manner the rights whatsoever of any states or any peoples or the terms of existing international instruments to which Members of the United Nations may respectively be parties.

2. Paragraph 1 of this Article shall not be interpreted as giving grounds for delay or postponement of the negotiation and conclusion of agreements for placing mandated and other territories under the trusteeship system as provided for in Article 77.

A R T I C L E 8 1

The trusteeship agreement shall in each case include the terms under which the trust territory will be administered and designate the authority which will exercise the administration of the trust territory. Such authority, hereinafter called the administering authority, may be one or more states or the Organization itself.

A R T I C L E 8 2

There may be designated, in any trusteeship agreement, a strategic area or areas which may include part or all of the trust territory to which the agreement applies, without prejudice to any special agreement or agreements made under Article 43.

A R T I C L E 8 3

1. All functions of the United Nations relating to strategic areas,

including the approval of the terms of the trusteeship agreements and of their alteration or amendment, shall be exercised by the Security Council.

2. The basic objectives set forth in Article 76 shall be applicable to the people of each strategic area.

3. The Security Council shall, subject to the provisions of the trusteeship agreements and without prejudice to security considerations, avail itself of the assistance of the Trusteeship Council to perform those functions of the United Nations under the trusteeship system relating to political, economic, social, and educational matters in the strategic areas.

A R T I C L E 8 4

It shall be the duty of the administering authority to ensure that the trust territory shall play its part in the maintenance of international peace and security. To this end the administering authority may make use of volunteer forces, facilities, and assistance from the trust territory in carrying out the obligations towards the Security Council undertaken in this regard by the administering authority, as well as for local defense and the maintenance of law and order within the trust territory.

A R T I C L E 8 5

1. The functions of the United Nations with regard to trusteeship agreements for all areas not designated as strategic, including the approval of the terms of the trusteeship agreements and of their alteration or amendment, shall be exercised by the General Assembly.

2. The Trusteeship Council, operating under the authority of the General Assembly, shall assist the General Assembly in carrying out these functions.

C H A P T E R 1 3

The Trusteeship Council

Composition

A R T I C L E 8 6

1. The Trusteeship Council shall consist of the following Members of the United Nations:

a. those Members administering trust territories;

b. such of those Members mentioned by name in Article 23 as are not administering trust territories; and

c. as many other Members elected for three-year terms by the General Assembly as may be necessary to ensure that the total number of members of the Trusteeship Council is equally divided between those Members of the United Nations which administer trust territories and those which do not.

2. Each member of the Trusteeship Council shall designate one specially qualified person to represent it therein.

Functions and Powers

ARTICLE 87

The General Assembly and, under its authority, the Trusteeship Council, in carrying out their functions, may:

a. consider reports submitted by the administering authority;

b. accept petitions and examine them in consultation with the administering authority;

c. provide for periodic visits to the respective trust territories at times agreed upon with the administering authority; and

d. take these and other actions in conformity with the terms of the trusteeship agreements.

ARTICLE 88

The Trusteeship Council shall formulate a questionnaire on the political, economic, social, and educational advancement of the inhabitants of each trust territory, and the administering authority for each trust territory within the competence of the General Assembly shall make an annual report to the General Assembly upon the basis of such questionnaire.

Voting

ARTICLE 89

1. Each member of the Trusteeship Council shall have one vote.

2. Decisions of the Trusteeship Council shall be made by a majority of the members present and voting.

Procedure

A R T I C L E 9 0

1. The Trusteeship Council shall adopt its own rules of procedure, including the method of selecting its President.

2. The Trusteeship Council shall meet as required in accordance with its rules, which shall include provision for the convening of meetings on the request of a majority of its members.

A R T I C L E 9 1

The Trusteeship Council shall, when appropriate, avail itself of the assistance' of the Economic and Social Council and of the specialized agencies in regard to matters with which they are respectively concerned.

C H A P T E R 1 4

The International Court of Justice

A R T I C L E 9 2

The International Court of Justice shall be the principal judicial organ of the United Nations. It shall function in accordance with the annexed Statute, which is based upon the Statute of the Permanent Court of International Justice and forms an integral part of the present Charter.

A R T I C L E 9 3

1. All Members of the United Nations are *ipso facto* parties to the Statute of the International Court of Justice.

2. A state which is not a Member of the United Nations may become a party to the Statute of the International Court of Justice on conditions to be determined in each case by the General Assembly upon the recommendation of the Security Council.

A R T I C L E 9 4

1. Each Member of the United Nations undertakes to comply with the decision of the International Court of Justice in any case to which it is a party.

2. If any party to a case fails to perform the obligations incumbent

upon it under a judgment rendered by the Court, the other party may have recourse to the Security Council, which may, if it deems necessary, make recommendations or decide upon measures to be taken to give effect to the judgment.

ARTICLE 95

Nothing in the present Charter shall prevent Members of the United Nations from entrusting the solution of their differences to other tribunals by virtue of agreements already in existence or which may be concluded in the future.

ARTICLE 96

1. The General Assembly or the Security Council may request the International Court of Justice to give an advisory opinion on any legal question.

2. Other organs of the United Nations and specialized agencies, which may at any time be so authorized by the General Assembly, may also request advisory opinions of the Court on legal questions arising within the scope of their activities.

CHAPTER 15

The Secretariat

ARTICLE 97

The Secretariat shall comprise a Secretary-General and such staff as the Organization may require. The Secretary-General shall be appointed by the General Assembly upon the recommendation of the Security Council. He shall be the chief administrative officer of the Organization.

ARTICLE 98

The Secretary-General shall act in that capacity in all meetings of the General Assembly, of the Security Council, of the Economic and Social Council, and of the Trusteeship Council, and shall perform such other functions as are entrusted to him by these organs. The Secretary-General shall make an annual report to the General Assembly on the work of the Organization.

A R T I C L E   9 9

The Secretary-General may bring to the attention of the Security Council any matter which in his opinion may threaten the maintenance of international peace and security.

A R T I C L E   1 0 0

1. In the performance of their duties the Secretary-General and the staff shall not seek or receive instructions from any government or from any other authority external to the Organization. They shall refrain from any action which might reflect on their position as international officials responsible only to the Organization.

2. Each Member of the United Nations undertakes to respect the exclusively international character of the responsibilities of the Secretary-General and the staff and not to seek to influence them in the discharge of their responsibilities.

A R T I C L E   1 0 1

1. The staff shall be appointed by the Secreteary-General under regulations established by the General Assembly.

2. Appropriate staffs shall be permanently assigned to the Economic and Social Council, the Trusteeship Council, and, as required, to other organs of the United Nations. These staffs shall form a part of the Secretariat.

3. The paramount consideration in the employment of the staff and in the determination of the conditions of service shall be the necessity of securing the highest standards of efficiency, competence, and integrity. Due regard shall be paid to the importance of recruiting the staff on as wide a geographical basis as possible.

C H A P T E R   1 6

Miscellaneous Provisions

A R T I C L E   1 0 2

1. Every treaty and every international agreement entered into by any Member of the United Nations after the present Charter comes into force shall as soon as possible be registered with the Secretariat and published by it.

2. No party to any such treaty or international agreement which has

not been registered in accordance with the provisions of paragraph 1 of this Article may invoke that treaty or agreement before any organ of the United Nations.

ARTICLE 103

In the event of a conflict between the obligations of the Members of the United Nations under the present Charter and their obligations under any other international agreement, their obligations under the present Charter shall prevail.

ARTICLE 104

The Organization shall enjoy in the territory of each of its Members such legal capacity as may be necessary for the exercise of its functions and the fulfillment of its purposes.

ARTICLE 105

1. The Organization shall enjoy in the territory of each of its Members such privileges and immunities as are necessary for the fulfillment of its purposes.

2. Representatives of the Members of the United Nations and officials of the Organization shall similarly enjoy such privileges and immunities as are necessary for the independent exercise of their functions in connection with the Organization.

3. The General Assembly may make recommendations with a view to determining the details of the application of paragraphs 1 and 2 of this Article or may propose conventions to the Members of the United Nations for this purpose.

CHAPTER 17

Transitional Security Arrangements

ARTICLE 106

Pending the coming into force of such special agreements referred to in Article 43 as in the opinion of the Security Council enable it to begin the exercise of its responsibilities under Article 42, the parties to the Four-Nation Declaration, signed at Moscow, October 30, 1943, and France, shall, in accordance with the provisions of paragraph 5 of that Declaration, consult with one another and as occasion requires with other Members of the United Nations with a view to such joint action on behalf of the Organization as may be necessary for the purpose of maintaining international peace and security.

ARTICLE 107

Nothing in the present Charter shall invalidate or preclude action, in relation to any state which during the Second World War has been an enemy of any signatory to the present Charter, taken or authorized as a result of that war by the Governments having responsibility for such action.

CHAPTER 18

Amendments

ARTICLE 108

Amendments to the present Charter shall come into force for all Members of the United Nations when they have been adopted by a vote of two thirds of the members of the General Assembly and ratified in accordance with their respective constitutional processes by two thirds of the Members of the United Nations, including all the permanent members of the Security Council.

ARTICLE 109

1. A General Conference of the Members of the United Nations for the purpose of reviewing the present Charter may be held at a date and place to be fixed by a two-thirds vote of the members of the General Assembly and by a vote of any seven* members of the Security Council. Each Member of the United Nations shall have one vote in the conference.

2. Any alteration of the present Charter recommended by a two-thirds vote of the conference shall take effect when ratified in accordance with their respective constitutional processes by two-thirds of the Members of the United Nations including all the permanent members of the Security Council.

3. If such a conference has not been held before the tenth annual session of the General Assembly following the coming into force of the present Charter, the proposal to call such a conference shall be placed

*See Note, p. 192.

on the agenda of that session of the General Assembly, and the conference shall be held if so decided by a majority vote of the members of the General Assembly and by a vote of any seven members of the Security Council.

CHAPTER 19

Ratification and Signature

ARTICLE 110

1. The present Charter shall be ratified by the signatory states in accordance with their respective constitutional processes.

2. The ratifications shall be deposited with the Government of the United States of America, which shall notify all the signatory states of each deposit as well as the Secretary-General of the Organization when he has been appointed.

3. The present Charter shall come into force upon the deposit of ratifications by the Republic of China, France, the Union of Soviet Socialist Republics, the United Kingdom of Great Britain and Northern Ireland, and the United States of America, and by a majority of the other signatory states. A protocol of the ratifications deposited shall thereupon be drawn up by the Government of the United States of America which shall communicate copies thereof to all the signatory states.

4. The states signatory to the present Charter which ratify it after it has come into force will become original Members of the United Nations on the date of the deposit of their respective ratifications.

ARTICLE 111

The present Charter, of which the Chinese, French, Russian, English, and Spanish texts are equally authentic, shall remain deposited in the archives of the Government of the United States of America. Duly certified copies thereof shall be transmitted by that Government to the Governments of the other signatory states.

IN FAITH WHEREOF the representatives of the Governments of the United Nations have signed the present Charter.

DONE at the city of San Francisco the twenty-sixth day of June, one thousand nine hundred and forty-five.

Universal Declaration of Human Rights

Approved by the General Assembly at its Plenary Meeting on

10 December 1948

P R E A M B L E

WHEREAS recognition of the inherent dignity and of the equal and inalienable rights of all members of the human family is the foundation of freedom, justice and peace in the world,

WHEREAS disregard and contempt for human rights have resulted in barbarous acts which have outraged the conscience of mankind, and the advent of a world in which human beings shall enjoy freedom of speech and belief and freedom from fear and want has been proclaimed as the highest aspiration of the common people,

WHEREAS it is essential, if man is not to be compelled to have recourse, as a last resort, to rebellion against tyranny and oppression, that human rights should be protected by the rule of law,

WHEREAS it is essential to promote the development of friendly relations between nations,

WHEREAS the peoples of the United Nations have in the Charter reaffirmed their faith in fundamental human rights, in the dignity and worth of the human person and in the equal rights of men and women and have determined to promote social progress and better standards of life in larger freedom,

WHEREAS Member States have pledged themselves to achieve, in co-operation with the United Nations, the promotion of universal respect for and observance of human rights and fundamental freedoms,

WHEREAS a common understanding of these rights and freedoms is of the greatest importance for the full realization of this pledge,

Now therefore

The General Assembly,

Proclaims this Universal Declaration of Human Rights as a common standard of achievement for all peoples and all nations, to the end that every individual and every organ of society, keeping this Declaration constantly in mind, shall strive by teaching and education to promote respect for these rights and freedoms and by progressive measures, national and international, to secure their universal and effective recognition and observance, both among the peoples of Member States themselves and among the peoples of territories under their jurisdiction.

A R T I C L E 1

All human beings are born free and equal in dignity and rights. They are endowed with reason and conscience and should act towards one another in a spirit of brotherhood.

A R T I C L E 2

Everyone is entitled to all the rights and freedoms set forth in this Declaration, without distinction of any kind, such as race, colour, sex, language, religion, political or other opinion, national or social origin, property, birth or other status.

Furthermore, no distinction shall be made on the basis of the political, jurisdictional or international status of the country or territory to which a person belongs, whether it be independent, trust, non-self-governing or under any other limitation of sovereignty.

A R T I C L E 3

Everyone has the right to life, liberty and the security of person.

A R T I C L E 4

No one shall be held in slavery or servitude; slavery and the slave trade shall be prohibited in all their forms.

A R T I C L E 5

No one shall be subjected to torture or to cruel, inhuman or degrading treatment or punishment.

A R T I C L E 6

Everyone has the right to recognition everywhere as a person before the law.

A R T I C L E 7

All are equal before the law and are entitled without any discrimination to equal protection of the law. All are entitled to equal protection against any discrimination in violation of this Declaration and against any incitement to such discrimination.

A R T I C L E 8

Everyone has the right to an effective remedy by the competent national tribunals for acts violating the fundamental rights granted him by the constitution or by law.

A R T I C L E 9

No one shall be subjected to arbitrary arrest, detention or exile.

A R T I C L E 1 0

Everyone is entitled in full equality to a fair and public hearing by an independent and impartial tribunal, in the determination of his rights and obligations and of any criminal charge against him.

A R T I C L E 1 1

1. Everyone charged with a penal offence has the right to be presumed innocent until proved guilty according to law in a public trial at which he has had all the guarantees necessary for his defence.

2. No one shall be held guilty of any penal offence on account of any act or omission which did not constitute a penal offence, under national or international law, at the time when it was committed. Nor shall a heavier penalty be imposed than the one that was applicable at the time the penal offence was committed.

ARTICLE 12

No one shall be subjected to arbitrary interference with his privacy, family, home or correspondence, nor to attacks upon his honour and reputation. Everyone has the right to the protection of the law against such interference or attacks.

ARTICLE 13

1. Everyone has the right to freedom of movement and residence within the borders of each state.

2. Everyone has the right to leave any country, including his own, and to return to his country.

ARTICLE 14

1. Everyone has the right to seek and to enjoy in other countries asylum from persecution.

2. This right may not be invoked in the case of prosecutions genuinely arising from non-political crimes or from acts contrary to the purposes and principles of the United Nations.

ARTICLE 15

1. Everyone has the right to a nationality.

2. No one shall be arbitrarily deprived of his nationality nor denied the right to change his nationality.

ARTICLE 16

1. Men and women of full age, without any limitation due to race, nationality or religion, have the right to marry and to found a family. They are entitled to equal rights as to marriage, during marriage and at its dissolution.

2. Marriage shall be entered into only with the free and full consent of the intending spouses.

3. The family is the natural and fundamental group unit of society and is entitled to protection by society and the State.

ARTICLE 17

1. Everyone has the right to own property alone as well as in association with others.

2. No one shall be arbitrarily deprived of his property.

ARTICLE 18

Everyone has the right to freedom of thought, conscience and religion; this right includes freedom to change his religion or belief, and freedom, either alone or in community with others and in public or private, to manifest his religion or belief in teaching, practice, worship and observance.

ARTICLE 19

Everyone has the right to freedom of opinion and expression; this right includes freedom to hold opinions without interference and to seek, receive and impart information and ideas through any media and regardless of frontiers.

ARTICLE 20

1. Everyone has the right to freedom of peaceful assembly and association.

2. No one may be compelled to belong to an association.

ARTICLE 21

1. Everyone has the right to take part in the Government of his country, directly or through freely chosen representatives.

2. Everyone has the right of equal access to public service in his country.

3. The will of the people shall be the basis of the authority of government; this will shall be expressed in periodic and genuine elections which shall be by universal and equal suffrage and shall be held by secret vote or by equivalent free voting procedures.

ARTICLE 22

Everyone, as a member of society, has the right to social security and is entitled to realization, through national effort and international cooperation and in accordance with the organization and resources of each State, of the economic, social and cultural rights indispensable for his dignity and the free development of his personality.

ARTICLE 23

1. Everyone has the right to work, to free choice of employment, to just and favourable conditions of work and to protection against unemployment.

2. Everyone, without any discrimination, has the right to equal pay for equal work.

3. Everyone who works has the right to just and favourable remuneration insuring for himself and his family an existence worthy of human dignity, and supplemented, if necessary, by other means of social protection.

4. Everyone has the right to form and to join trade unions for the protection of his interests.

ARTICLE 24

Everyone has the right to rest and leisure, including reasonable limitation of working hours and periodic holidays with pay.

ARTICLE 25

1. Everyone has the right to a standard of living adequate for the health and well-being of himself and of his family, including food, clothing, housing and medical care and necessary social services, and the right to security in the event of unemployment, sickness, disability, widowhood, old age or other lack of livelihood in circumstances beyond his control.

2. Motherhood and childhood are entitled to special care and assistance. All children, whether born in or out of wedlock, shall enjoy the same social protection.

ARTICLE 26

1. Everyone has the right to education. Education shall be free, at least in the elementary and fundamental stages. Elementary education shall be compulsory. Technical and professional education shall be made generally available and higher education shall be equally accessible to all on the basis of merit.

2. Education shall be directed to the full development of the human personality and to the strengthening of respect for human rights and fundamental freedoms. It shall promote understanding, tolerance and friendship among all nations, racial or religious groups, and shall further the activities of the United Nations for the maintenance of peace.

3. Parents have a prior right to choose the kind of education that shall be given to their children.

ARTICLE 27

1. Everyone has the right freely to participate in the cultural life of the community, to enjoy the arts and to share in scientific advancement and its benefits.

2. Everyone has the right to the protection of the moral and material interests resulting from any scientific, literary or artistic production of which he is the author.

ARTICLE 28

Everyone is entitled to a social and international order in which the rights and freedoms set forth in this Declaration can be fully realized.

ARTICLE 29

1. Everyone has duties to the community in which alone the free and full development of his personality is possible.

2. In the exercise of his rights and freedoms, everyone shall be subject only to such limitations as are determined by law solely for the purpose of securing due recognition and respect for the rights and freedoms of others and of meeting the just requirements of morality, public order and the general welfare in a democratic society.

3. These rights and freedoms may in no case be exercised contrary to the purposes and principles of the United Nations.

ARTICLE 30

Nothing in this Declaration may be interpreted as implying for any State, group or person any right to engage in any activity or to perform any act aimed at the destruction of any of the rights and freedoms set forth herein.

Sources

1 Remarks to the United Nations Correspondents Association, July 10, 1953.
2 Press conference at United Nations Headquarters, May 5, 1960.
3 Press conference transcript, Canberra, Australia, February 14, 1956.
4 Press conference transcript, Djakarta, Indonesia, February 12, 1956.
5 Address to the staff of the United Nations Office at the Palais des Nations, Geneva, May 26, 1953.
6 Address before a meeting of the Norwegian Association for the United Nations at the Festival Hall, University of Oslo, June 3, 1958.
7 Press conference transcript, April 30, 1959.
8 Extemporaneous remarks before the Indian Council of World Affairs in New Delhi, India, February 3, 1956. Edited and corrected transcript.
9 Address at the Special Convocation and dedicatory celebration marking the completion and occupancy of the law buildings of the University of Chicago Law School, Chicago, May 1, 1960.
10 Address before the Students Association, Copenhagen, Denmark, May 2, 1959.
11 Address at a luncheon at Cambridge University, Cambridge, England, June 5, 1958.

232

12 Address at the state dinner of the 50th Annual Meeting of the Governors Conference, Miami, Florida, May 19, 1958.

13 Address to a meeting of Members of both Houses of Parliament under the auspices of the British Group of the Inter-Parliamentary Union, London, April 2, 1958.

14 Address before the Economics Club of New York, March 1960.

15 Statement on his reelection to a second term, before the General Assembly, September 26, 1957.

16 Statement at the second session of the United Nations Economic Commission for Africa at Tangier, Morocco, January 1960.

17 Introduction to the Secretary-General's fourteenth annual report to the General Assembly on the work of the Organization from June 16, 1958, to June 15, 1959.

18 Introduction to the Secretary-General's fifteenth annual report to the General Assembly on the work of the Organization from June 16, 1959, to June 15, 1960.

19 Introduction to the Secretary-General's sixteenth annual report to the General Assembly on the work of the Organization from June 16, 1960, to June 15, 1961.

20 Statement to the press on arrival at International Airport, New York, April 9, 1953.

21 Statement before the Plenary Session of the General Assembly, April 10, 1953, after his election as Secretary-General.

22 Address at luncheon given by the American Political Science Association, Washington, D.C., September 11, 1953.

23 Address at dinner in his honor given by the American Association for the United Nations in cooperation with the New York University Institute for Review of United Nations Affairs, New York, September 14, 1953.

24 Address to the Foreign Policy Association at a dinner given in his honor, New York, October 21, 1953.

25 Address before the Second Assembly of the World Council of Churches, Evanston, Illinois, August 20, 1954.

26 Address at Johns Hopkins University commencement exercises, Baltimore, Maryland, June 14, 1955.

27 Commencement address at Stanford University, Palo Alto, California, June 19, 1955.

28 Address at University of California United Nations Convocation, Berkeley, California, June 25, 1955.

49 Press conference transcript, February 4, 1960.

50 Press conference transcript, June 2, 1960.

51 Statement dated June 6, 1960, circulated to members of the Economic and Social Council in advance of its annual debate on the world economic situation at the thirtieth session beginning in Geneva the following month.

52 Statement before the General Assembly in reply to Chairman Khrushchev, September 26, 1960.

53 Statement to the General Assembly, October 3, 1960.

54 Statement before the Security Council, December 7, 1960.

55 Statement before the Security Council, February 17, 1961.

56 Lecture delivered to the Congregation at Oxford University, May 30, 1961.

57 Press conference transcript, June 12, 1961.

58 Last speech made to the Secretariat staff on the occasion of Staff Day in the General Assembly Hall, September 8, 1961, ten days before his tragic death.

59 Statement at the United Nations Day Concert, October 24, 1960. Rebroadcast eleven months later during the memorial ceremony in the General Assembly Hall for him and those who died with him in the Ndola forest.

60 Press conference in New Delhi, February 5, 1956.

61 Press conference at United Nations Headquarters, June 26, 1961.

62 Press conference in Teheran, Iran, January 26, 1956.

63 Press conference held in Karachi, Pakistan, January 31, 1956.

64 Press conference at United Nations Headquarters, February 4, 1960.

65 United Nations Correspondents Association Luncheon in New York, March 8, 1956.

66 Press conference transcript, Israel, January 1956.

67 Press conference transcript, Rangoon, Burma, February 8, 1956.

68 Statement before the Security Council at the conclusion of the debate on the Congo, December 13, 1960.

69 "International Zone" United Nations-television program number 12, Alistair Cooke host, released October 1961, after Hammarskjöld's death.

70 Statement before the General Assembly, October 17, 1960.

71 Statement on the occasion of the rededication of the Memorial

Plaque for Count Folke Bernadotte at United Nations Headquarters, July 24, 1953.

72 Statement at the unveiling of the Lord Cecil Memorial at the Palais des Nations in Geneva, July 11, 1961.

73 Statement at the occasion of the Human Rights Day Concert in the General Assembly Hall, December 10, 1960.

74 Statement before the General Assembly, April 5, 1961, in answer to Soviet Foreign Minister Andrei Gromyko.

75 Interview by the Burmese Broadcasting Service, Rangoon, February 1956.

76 Introduction to the Secretary-General's annual report to the General Assembly on the work of the Organization, 1952–1953.

77 Introduction to the Secretary-General's annual report to the General Assembly on the work of the Organization, 1953–1954.

78 Introduction to the Secretary-General's annual report to the General Assembly on the work of the Organization, 1954–1955.

79 Statement written for "This I Believe," Edward R. Murrow's radio program.

80 Address before the Academic Association of the University of Lund, Lund, Sweden, May 4, 1959.

81 Inaugural address upon taking the seat as a member of the Swedish Academy, Stockholm, December 20, 1954.

82 Television press conference, Canadian Broadcasting Corporation, March 7, 1956.

83 *Markings* (New York: Alfred A. Knopf, 1964).